AN ORCHARD ODYSSEY

AN
ORCHARD
ODYSSEY

Find and grow tree fruit in your garden, community and beyond

Naomi Slade

Published by
Green Books
An imprint of UIT Cambridge Ltd
www.greenbooks.co.uk

PO Box 145, Cambridge CB4 1GQ, England
+44 (0)1223 302 041

First published in 2017, in England

Naomi Slade has asserted her moral rights under the Copyright, Designs and Patents Act 1988.

The front cover shows the National Trust's Greys Court, near Henley-on-Thames, in autumn. Photograph © Naomi Slade.

All interior photographs are by the author, with the exception of the following. Page 7: © Patrick Drummond. Page 34: © Eric Sander. Page 36: © David Daniels. Page 47: © Oxford University Images / Joby Sessions (2015). Pages 50, 118 (right): © Morwenna Slade. Page 75: © Li Brookman. Pages 80, 108, 119, 178 (left): © The Urban Orchard Project. Pages 88 (left), 186 (bottom middle): © Royal Horticultural Society. Page 103: courtesy of Tom Burford. Page 129: © Jason Ingram. Pages 187, 190, 197 (bottom left): © Chris Wlaznik. Page 199 (left): © Suttons. Artworks on pages 37, 44, 56, 67, 83, 95, 96, 99, 111, 121, 127: Shutterstock.

The publishers have endeavoured to identify all copyright holders, but will be glad to correct in future editions any omissions brought to their notice.

Design by Jayne Jones

ISBN: 978-0-85784-326-5 (hardback)
ISBN: 978-0-85784-327-2 (ePub)
ISBN: 978-0-85784-328-9 (pdf)
Also available for Kindle

Disclaimer: the advice herein is believed to be correct at the time of printing, but the author and publisher accept no liability for actions inspired by this book.

10 9 8 7 6 5 4 3 2 1

MIX
Paper from responsible sources
FSC® C016779
www.fsc.org

CONTENTS

To Dr John Slade, my botanical uncle

ACKNOWLEDGEMENTS

I would like to thank Chris Wlaznik and Morwenna Slade for their energy, inspiration and steadfastness: without them this book would not exist. And my children, for the times they had to make their own tea and for their willingness to pick fruit and embrace the adventure. Thanks to my parents, Marilyn and Roger, for support and encouragement. And to Uncle Johnny for all the trees.

For their rigorous proof-check and brilliant ideas, Rose Ward, Michelle Chapman and Janet Angus must be gratefully acknowledged, as must Danny and Sheila Daniels, whose pursuit of *Streuobstwiesen* went beyond the call of duty. Thanks to James Wong for crafting a sparkly foreword and to Andreas von Einsiedel for the shiny author photograph.

I am grateful to all the people I met along the road. The National Trust at Canons Ashby, Greys Court and West Green House; the many, and unstintingly kind, National Gardens Scheme garden owners, the Royal Horticultural Society, The Urban Orchard Project, the Kensington Roof Garden, Jason Ingram, Eric Sander and everyone else who was generous with images, information, locations and interviews. And, notably, the providers of context and stories – the garden owners, juice-makers, orchard experts, horticulturists and random passers-by. Those who let me loose, gave me their time, told their tales and posed for pictures; the organizations and individuals across the world who responded with delightful generosity to being doorstepped for information.

Finally, my thanks must go to the team at Green Books: Niall and Sheila, Lindsey, Alethea and Jayne, for their magic touch.

FOREWORD

All over the world, small traditional orchards are under threat. Even in small domestic gardens, the enthusiasm for cultivating vegetables has far outstripped that for fruit. It seems fruit trees are mistakenly seen as being too big, too complex and unrewarding for modern gardeners. This book is the first step to changing all that. Preserving orchards is about so much more than bucolic nostalgia: if we lose orchards from our landscape, we lose not only a part of our heritage but also vital habitats for wildlife and a vast genetic repository that has taken thousands of years to develop.

Ditching the dusty tables of compatible varieties and pages of tortuous pruning advice of many of its predecessors, this is the first book I know to address the *why* of orchard growing as much as the *how*. Why are they so fascinating? Why are they under threat? Why is it so important we preserve them? I found this book fuzzily absorbing, like a horticultural fairytale. It tells of the rich history of orchards; of fascinating people, plants and places to inspire the reader. Yet, crucially, it also provides a practical roadmap to actually getting started – even in the increasingly tiny modern garden.

Spot a tree in the landscape and understand how it got there, with the eye-opening tips found in these pages. Learn to plan, plant and maintain an orchard on any scale. Uncover the vital role orchards will play in the twenty-first century. Naomi has created an encyclopedic yet accessible resource for both novices and veterans, enabling us to re-engage with both why orchards are so vital and how to ensure their survival. Well done.

James Wong

INTRODUCTION

Orchards delight me. Exciting and compelling in their infinite variety and character, they speak to me on a fundamental level. I am intrigued by their history and folklore, and I love the embodiment of an eco-system that is both stable and ancient. Amongst the trees – the insects gently pollinating, the birds in the branches, the fruit quietly swelling in its own good time – that is how it has been forever: peaceful and timeless.

In the depths of winter, the sight of a stray tree, still full of big yellow apples, is uplifting. A romantic confetti of blossom heralds each spring: first plum, then apple flowers, like bunches of miniature blush roses. The fruit-bright autumn roadside is a mystery of semi-wilderness; a miscellany of trees planted as named varieties and 'wildings' that have sprung from discarded cores.

When the orchards at home are laden with their beautiful crop, dappled in sunlight or softened by mist, there is nowhere else I would rather be. They entice me to find a basket and get picking, to climb a ladder to the very top and swing there between the trees and the sky in the hope of reaching the highest, most perfect apples.

Fallen apples lie on the ground in late winter.

THE TRADITIONAL ORCHARD

Orchards have been a major feature of the landscape for centuries. Embedded in the collective psyche, they have huge social and cultural significance. They are filled with tradition and local colour and are singularly important for wildlife.

Time was that the orchard was part of the community. Every cottage would have a tree or two; every farm and country house would have a collection of fruit trees, however modest. They would provide food for family and workers: apples to eat fresh, to use in pies, to eat with savouries or to enjoy roasted in warmed ale and winter punches. Pigs and cattle would graze beneath the trees and there might be hay or mistletoe to cut. The trees would be wassailed in January to ensure a good crop that year, and harvested in late summer and autumn. They were part of life.

In the latter half of the twentieth century many traditional orchards were destroyed, while others are now succumbing to neglect and simply fading away. There is, perhaps, a feeling that their time is past; that this is a nostalgic idyll which, with our busy lives and high-rise lifestyles, we can only dream of restoring or enjoying.

The love of orchards has not diminished, but even in the countryside people have grown further from the reality. Collections of beautiful fruit trees are viewed with a retrospective melancholy. There is a sense that, although they have existence value, they are not relevant to contemporary life. A feeling that orchards are now out of reach, part of an unattainable tradition that has, regretfully, been relegated to a rural museum piece.

This garden has grown up around its fruit trees.

I disagree. And I believe that there needs to be a paradigm shift.

Traditional orchards are often defined for conservation as just 'a minimum of five fruit or nut trees, with canopy edges not more than 20m (66') apart'. Yet this covers virtually every scenario. From modern patio fruit to fragments of ancient orchard, this simple definition can be adopted to encompass almost every garden size and budget.

Choose the right fruit varieties on the right rootstock, take into consideration the space available, and the very smallest garden can have an orchard. Perhaps not with an integral hay meadow and ancient hedgeline, but an orchard nonetheless. The trees don't have to be 20m apart; dwarf or containerized trees can be as little as 1m (3') apart. They don't have to be laid out in rows in a field; they can work as formal planting, framing a doorway, edging a path or in containers descending a flight of steps. They can be trained as a fan or espalier, or planted in a border full of flowers. They don't have to be grazed by pigs; a lawnmower will do.

The concept of 'orchard' needs to be repurposed; a parallel narrative developed that takes into account how we live today. We need a twenty-first-century approach to orchard gardening. The principle of grow-your-own, hugely popular with vegetables, applies just as well to tree fruit.

In towns, extended 'orchards' already exist. Applying the five-trees rule and ignoring artificial boundaries, there are many landscapes in which fruit is planted in a loose orchard continuum – and there is plenty of room for more. Trees growing alongside flowers and shrubs, the grass lightly mown, wildlife generally encouraged – this fits comfortably amongst dwellings and in townscapes. And, where such planting is sparse, subtle changes can easily draw it nearer.

Although a tiny garden may not have room for beetle-friendly standing deadwood, a choice of historic local fruit varieties will help to conserve the regional heritage, and the bees and butterflies will thank you for them. The wide range of standard, dwarf and trained fruit can accommodate all design tastes. And there is no reason why you can't wassail the apple trees in an urban back garden.

ORCHARDS FOR ALL

Demands are changing. People are actively seeking out new flavours and new varieties of food, and embracing differences in the character of what they eat. There is an increased understanding of seasonality and food miles, and of the need for conservation. There are concerns about food security, production methods and provenance. In this context, orchard gardening can be relevant and desirable again. Indeed, it is not just relevant but achievable, and brings clear benefits not only to the individual and the environment but also potentially to the local economy and community.

Decorative and flavoursome, fruit holds its own in the garden.

New orchard gardening

Leave aside, for a moment, the vision of acres of commercially cropping trees and of standard trees the size of a double garage; the fear of gluts and of obscure terminology. Think small. Think unique. Take a new look at what you have. Where do you live? What do you like? How much space do you have? How many people do you feed?

New orchard gardening is all about informed choice. And it is not all about apples and pears. If there is space against a wall or fence, then fan-trained cherries or apricots might be an option. Lemon and olive trees are an attractive addition to a smart patio. Expensive treats, like plums and cherries, can be yours for the picking, or you could cultivate a taste for oddities.

Get to know the trees, and their distinctiveness will shine through. That upright character, the juicy fruit, the reassuring hardiness, the incredible aroma – that sudden blossom hit that signals spring. Discover the full

BELOW LEFT: Apples are objects of beauty and desire.

BELOW RIGHT: Fragrant lemon blossom.

palimpsest of character and individuality that thousands of years of local variation and selective breeding can bring. Have confidence in choosing and caring for the fruit trees you want, and in looking after what you have, in the context of your personal tastes and circumstances. Rediscover the joys of orchard gardening.

THE ORCHARD ODYSSEY

This is a book about embarking on a journey of fruit, a personal orchard odyssey through garden and landscape. It aims to whet the appetite with epic tales, to delight with nuggets of joy and to cast a new perspective on what orchard gardening is and means.

This book is created in the spirit of insatiable intellectual curiosity and the pleasure of discovery – not just the revelations of kitchen, garden and landscape, but also in the artistic perspective of literature and film. It revels in the frisson of geeky amusement at time-travelling fruit that turns up in the wrong era in historical films (in *Pirates of the Caribbean*, the heroine is offered a Granny Smith apple about 120 years before its actual discovery, while in the 2012 film *Mirror Mirror*, the apple that the evil queen is holding looks a lot like a not-terribly-ancient Red Delicious). Fruit plays a leitmotif role in human culture – from Chaucer being cheeky about medlars to a golden apple precipitating the Trojan War. *An Orchard Odyssey* proposes a revised and joyous connectedness with our fruity heritage.

So, what to do next? Anything you like: plant a plum, scrump an apple, start a fruit appreciation group. Wander around Europe eating jam. Create an online map of local varieties. Go outside and find 'your' tree.

Own your fruit, your hunger and your vision. To quote Henry David Thoreau, *"It is not what you look at that matters, it is what you see."*

HOW TO USE THIS BOOK

This book is a starting point. It is the point on a quest where the hero picks up his bag and walks through the door, into a bright morning full of possibilities.

Here you will find out about orchards and their history; will learn about the foibles of the fruit and how to spot trees that may be fruiting prolifically under your very nose. The book gives guidance on tree choice and explains the importance of orchards in the environment. It looks at their role in design and lifestyle; how they can be taken into the community and used as a force for social good. So it is a book of stories, but it is also a book of action – your action.

Not everyone's journey starts in the same place, so read the bits that interest you; those that are relevant, achievable or entertaining. This book is not, and does not pretend to be, a directory of fruit. While it includes practical advice on choosing trees, planting them and caring for them, and clarifies the technicalities of things like rootstocks, there are other tomes that concentrate exclusively on cultivation, which will make useful further reading. This book, meanwhile, sets the scene, advances an alternative perspective, and – I hope – inspires the next move.

If you want to find out more, look in the Resources section at the back. You could also do a little detective work in your own neighbourhood. Talk to people, eat and drink, share stories, see the sights. This is where the journey begins.

Notes on regions and seasons

I grow a lot of apples, and as a result the book talks a lot about apples – but when it comes to the big ideas, you can substitute the fruit of your choice. Orchards are highly individual, and you must apply the ideas to the orchards where you are. It is the concept that is important.

And, because this book aims to inspire a personal journey, specifics such as whether you are based in an urban or rural location, or even which country or hemisphere you occupy, aren't really relevant. Wherever the book is read, the chances are that fruit gardens will, in some form, be there too. There are school gardens in Brixton and in Hawaii; there are local apples in Poland and in East Anglia.

To keep things simple, when referring to the time of year I have used general terms rather than named months. These give a good indication of what happens when, but regional conditions vary, so always check with local sources of information too.

One final note: 'cider' refers to the alcoholic apple beverage known as 'hard cider' in the United States. Handle with care.

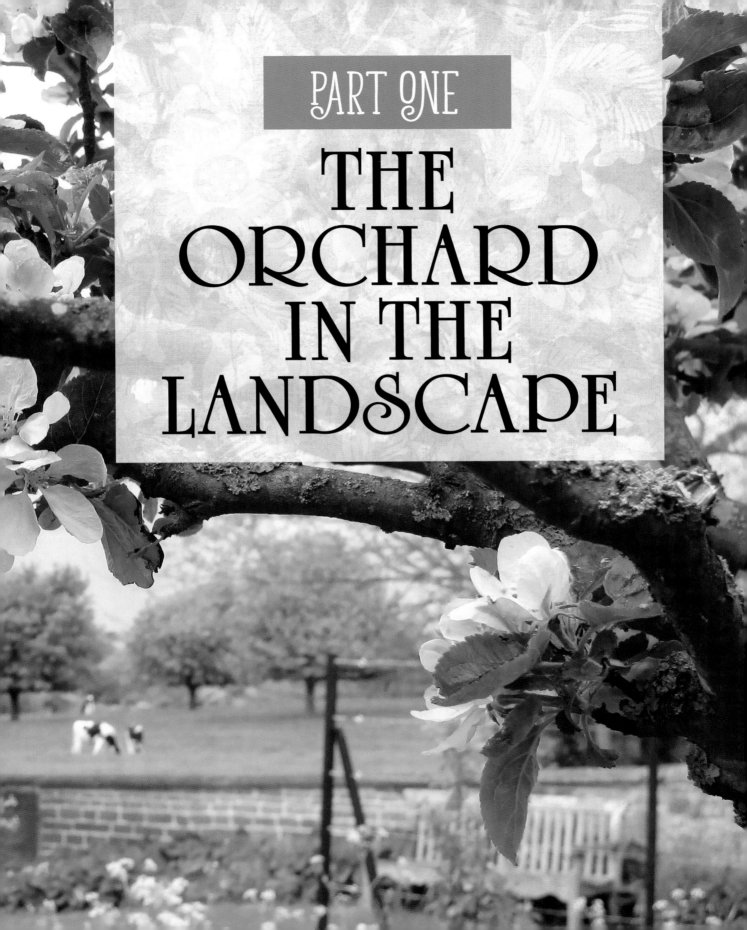

PART ONE

THE ORCHARD IN THE LANDSCAPE

CHAPTER ONE

FROM WILDERNESS TO CULTIVATION

Fruit-bearing trees are ubiquitous in our cultivated landscape, and yet their history goes back millions of years, to a place before human intervention. A place where the trees existed in the wilderness, evolving as a result of local environmental pressure in a natural explosion of diversity.

As an important food source, fruit was adopted early in human history. Since prehistoric times it has been consumed opportunistically and also traded. And, as varieties were brought into cultivation, techniques such as grafting and training were developed and disseminated. Fruit-growing has waxed and waned according to fashion and social and political need: some ideas and some cultivars have been wildly successful; others doomed to extinction. Farming practices have had an enormous impact. Today, fruit-growing is a multi-billion-pound industry, with continuous research and new developments every year.

The history of fruit is an epic tale. In cultivation, fruit has marched across the globe with humankind and also evolved independently of us. It has had a role in major human transitions, from nomadic tribes to agrarian settlers to an international community: monumental journeys in space, time and culture. But, as this book will reveal, each of us can also embark on a fruit-growing voyage of our own devising, much closer to home.

To put the present-day scene into context, this chapter looks at where tree fruit originated and how it became so commonplace across the world. It explores the ways in which it has been embraced and become significant, highlighting key points in the fruits' own history. It also charts the decline of orchards in the twentieth century, as modern farming methods and government drives for productivity took their toll.

The trees we find in our neighbourhoods and back gardens, the ones we see in hedgerows as we whizz past them in cars and trains, have roots in the distant past. And their orchard odyssey began long ago and far away.

OPPOSITE: After the petals fall, the pears show early promise.

BELOW: Harvest time in the orchard at RHS Garden Wisley, Surrey.

"But without the courtyard, hard by the door, is a great orchard of four acres, and a hedge runs about it on either side. Therein grow trees, tall and luxuriant, pears and pomegranates and apple-trees with their bright fruit, and sweet figs, and luxuriant olives. Of these the fruit perishes not nor fails in winter or in summer, but lasts throughout the year; and ever does the west wind, as it blows, quicken to life some fruits, and ripen others; pear upon pear waxes ripe, apple upon apple, cluster upon cluster, and fig upon fig . . . Such were the glorious gifts of the gods in the palace of Alcinous."
HOMER, *THE ODYSSEY*

THE ORIGIN OF APPLES

The apple is an iconic fruit. Indeed, apples *are* orchards to many people, so it is worth taking a look at where apples originated and how they migrated and diversified. This story begins about 4.5 million years ago, in the Tien Shan mountains on the border between China and Kazakhstan, with an isolated pocket of the Central Asian species of apple, known as *Malus sieversii*.

Under local selection pressures, these apples gradually began to change their seed-dispersal mechanism from birds to mammals. As the centuries passed, the fruit got bigger and juicier to tempt the native deer, pigs, bears and horses, while the seeds developed a tough outer case to withstand the longer digestive transit.

In the mountains of the East, a fruit forest grew. Tall trees and small ones; suckering on multiple stems or towering up to 18m (60') high; clinging to soaring mountains and nestling in deep ravines. Protected from glaciation by the warm winds of the Indian Ocean, the trees evolved without interruption. The more attractive the fruit became, the more the animals would seek it out. Brown bears preparing for hibernation would strive to get at the plumpest, sweetest apples. Fallen fruit eaten by horses would have its pips deposited, helpfully manured, well away from its parent. With the advantages conferred by these dispersal methods, the fruit became ever-more appealing and more diverse.

OPPOSITE: Sweet figs, the gifts of the gods.

-24-

The wild orchards of apples, growing alongside apricots, pears, nuts and cherry plums, reached from the mountains to the plains, where there arose the city of Almaty, a name derived from Alma-Ata: The Fatherland of the Apple.

Travelling companions

The eventual arrival of humans, with their insatiable hunger and wanderlust, heralded a new phase for fruiting species. Then, as now, no herdsman, trader, nomad or foraging urchin worth their salt would pass a decent meal, quite literally growing on trees, without helping themselves.

The Mongolian Plain to the north and the Gobi Desert to the east were inhospitable and, as civilizations developed and precious materials like lapis lazuli were traded from what is now Afghanistan to China and Egypt, merchants would take the easiest route west through the mountain passes – a route lined with tasty, nutritious nuggets of food.

Picked in the mountains and stashed in a saddle bag, the apples, together with plums pears, cherries and apricots, would travel some distance. The cores and pips discarded along the trail would grow into new trees. Thus, even before international trade or cultivation, the trees began to reach out from their mountain fastness along the human highways, their genes spreading, interweaving and diverging.

Evidence of East–West trade in fruit around 6,000 years ago, along what would later become the Silk Routes, was provided by the uncovering of Caucasian mummies in the Takla Makan Desert, south of the Tien Shan. Theories about the early trade and transport of apples are also supported by genetic detective work. In fact, for many years it was believed that the huge range of modern culinary and dessert apples had evolved from the small and thorny European crab apple, *Malus sylvestris*. But the work of Russian scientist Nikolai Vavilov (1887-1943), published in 1930, indicated that this was not the case, and when the Iron Curtain fell in the late twentieth century and the Eastern fruit forests were more widely 'discovered', DNA sequencing indicated that all our cultivated apples – historically thought to be hybrids of unknown parentage and referred to as *Malus x domestica* – had in fact arisen from the Asian 'Eve' population in the Tien Shan.

This has led to the assertion that the correct name for both the wild apple in the Tien Shan and our Western domestic apple is *Malus pumila*. Despite this, the wild Asian apple is usually known as *M. sieversii*, and the names *M. pumila* and *M. domestica* are both used, often interchangeably, for cultivated crops and their offspring.

COMPLEX GENOMES

When scientists sequenced the genome of the Golden Delicious apple, the results published in *Nature Genetics* in 2010, it proved to be the largest plant gene sequence ever discovered, and larger than the human genome. It is believed that this occurred as a result of duplication far back in the apple's evolutionary history, and that it gives the fruit a competitive advantage, enabling it to adapt effectively when faced with disease.

ORCHARD GARDENING THROUGH THE AGES

Traces of apple seeds have been found at settlements dating as far back as 6500 BC, and, as apples, pears and other fruit marched west, the written evidence for their presence increased. The cultivated offspring of the Asian *Malus sieversii*, along with other fruit species, gradually spread to the Middle East and then on to Greece and Rome, and there are records of Romans, Vikings, ancient Greeks and Persians eating apples.

APPLES IN THE NEW WORLD

Apples and pears spread from Europe to become a vast global industry.

In the sixteenth, seventeenth and eighteenth centuries, apples continued their inexorable march across the globe, using European explorers, missionaries, traders and settlers as a vector. The fruit jumped to the Americas with a panoply of northern Europeans. It got a foothold in the Eastern Seaboard and took the wagons of the Western pioneers to the Pacific. There, in the incomparable orchards of California, it met the progeny of fruit that had arrived in South America with the Spanish and Portuguese and then moved north with settlers and missionaries. (More on the story of apples in America on pages 41-5.)

The Dutchman Jan van Riebeeck, founder of the Netherlands East India Company's Cape Town trading arm, conveyed apples to South Africa in 1654, insisting that fruit was cultivated to feed the European settlers and supply eastbound ships. When, at the end of the nineteenth century, the grape harvest was devastated, the new British State of South Africa looked to a commercial alternative and laid the foundations of a bright future in apple-growing.

Meanwhile, in the Antipodes, with explorers and buccaneers circling the continent like sharks, 1788 was a big year for the introduction of fruit. Captain Arthur Phillip is credited with taking the first apple trees to Port Jackson, later to become Sydney, while Captain Bligh anchored the *Bounty* off Tasmania for long enough for the ship's botanist to plant apples and pears. With further settlements came further orchards, and in 1814 English missionaries set out to New Zealand, which they rapidly annexed for God, apples and Australia. They took with them the first fruit of what would become an established industry, ultimately creating varieties such as Royal Gala and Braeburn.

Collectively, the countries of the southern hemisphere took advantage of robust fruit that would travel well and, with their seasons complementing those of the north, South Africa, Australia, New Zealand, Chile, Argentina and Brazil became a formidable force in the global fruit market.

It is generally thought that the technique of grafting fruit to conserve and distribute chosen varieties also reached Rome via Persia and Greece, and that it was the Romans who then introduced cultivated and grafted fruit across Europe, from where it eventually reached the New World.

Cultivated fruit is believed to have arrived in England with the Romans and, although it declined during the Dark Ages as the country was battered by the Angles, Saxons and Jutes, these later invaders also left a scattering of place names, such as Applegarth, Appleby and Appleton, that hint at orchards past.

Medieval times saw a revival, as monasteries cultivated fruit and vegetables and raised funds by selling spiced cider. They also developed new varieties from cross-pollinated seedlings. Orchard gardening received a further boost following the Norman Conquest of 1066, as the Normans became prominent in the Church, bringing with them French traditions of apple-growing and cider-making, and further new varieties.

The name 'damson' derives from the Latin *Prunum damascenum,* or plum of Damascus.

THE FRUITS OF CONQUEST

The Normans introduced 'Costard' apples, which were first recorded in Britain in 1296. Sellers of this apple were known as costardmongers, and 'costermonger' is still used as a somewhat archaic term for a greengrocer or barrow-boy.

A BRIEF HISTORY OF PEARS

Pears were cultivated in China as early as 1000 BC.

Pears were all the rage in seventeenth-century France.

Pears come in many different forms, and the wild *Pyrus communis* is widely spread as a native of Europe and northern Asia. The fruit is small, hard and astringent – suitable for making perry but not so good for eating fresh.

By the thirteenth century, a hard, culinary pear was recorded as being grown at the Cistercian Abbey of Warden in Bedfordshire, and it has some claim to being the first named 'British' pear. Known as Wardens (Wardon, Wardoune), it has

been suggested that this might have been a variety also known as Black Worcester, which is still available today. Equally, the name could have referred to any long-keeping cooking pear that was used as a savoury addition to the winter diet.

By the mid-sixteenth century, over 50 varieties of pear were available, including the butter or *beurré* pears – which, unlike their predecessors, had soft, melting flesh. From this point the popularity of the pear grew. There was a craze for collecting pear varieties in seventeenth-century France, but it was a century later in Belgium that pear-breeding really took off, becoming a hobby for the well educated. The influence spread, and varieties that date from around this time include the Belgian cultivar Glou Morçeau and Williams' Bon Chrétien. Bred in Berkshire, England, Williams' Bon Chrétien was known as Bartlett in the USA, where it was the foundation of the canned pear industry. It is the most widely grown pear in the world.

For more information, see *The Book of Pears* by Joan Morgan, listed in Resources.

From the fourteenth century, orchards declined again, with the Black Death and later the Wars of the Roses. But in 1533 King Henry VIII commissioned royal fruiterer Richard Harris to plant experimental orchards in Kent, using grafts brought from France and Holland (see page 32). Hardy, tasty and disease-free varieties were distributed to other growers, revitalizing the industry. And, by the seventeenth century, most small farms in Britain and beyond would have had their own orchard and often also a cider press.

Fruit-growing in the Britain continued with modest popularity, and by the seventeenth century it was widely associated with the aristocracy. Influenced by Continental fruit fashions, orchards were gradually established in the grounds of large English houses – orchards that featured both restricted forms, à la Versailles, and the larger trees and spacious plantings that later came to be such a recognizable landscape feature. Towards the end of the eighteenth century, a series of pollination experiments by Thomas Andrew Knight in England and by other breeders in

Fruit-growing was popular with the aristocracy, even at relatively modest manors such as Canons Ashby in Northamptonshire.

RICHARD HARRIS AND KING HENRY VIII

Towards the end of the Middle Ages, diverse social turmoil saw a decline in fruit-growing, but English commercial orchards were revitalized in style by King Henry VIII. Soon after ascending the throne in 1509, he began a campaign to make Britain self-sufficient in fruit. In 1533, Richard Harris, fruiterer to the king, set up 105 acres (42 hectares) of orchards at Teynham in Kent.

Mainland Europe had a more robust culture of tree cultivation than England, and Harris looked to France and Holland for good-quality trees. With royal encouragement, he systematically acquired the best of French apple trees, returning with 'a great store of grafts' and concentrating particularly on pippins and other varieties from Normandy. He also liberally imported cherries, of which the king was particularly fond.

The trees at Teynham were propagated and passed on to other growers, which had a lasting impact on the regional landscape and agriculture. The legacy of Henry VIII, the orchard king, boosted apple consumption for several centuries after the end of his reign.

Henry VIII was particularly fond of cherries. His orchards must have been a wonderful sight in spring.

Belgium led to trees with improved fruit and influenced many subsequent pioneers. This was a golden age of horticulture, and new apples developed for taste appeared in their droves, including Cox's Orange Pippin, Egremont Russet and Worcester Pearmain.

In the nineteenth century, the Horticultural Society, later the Royal Horticultural Society (RHS), encouraged and rewarded apple- and pear-breeding. A catalogue first published in 1826 details over 1,400 apples and 677 pears (although some of these were later proved to be synonyms) in their gardens. This collection was followed by the National Fruit Trials. In 1989 it became the National Fruit Collection, located at Brogdale Farm and owned by the Department for Environment, Food & Rural Affairs (Defra). The charity Brogdale Collections is responsible for public access and events.

At RHS Garden Wisley, apples are harvested from September through to December.

LE POTAGER DU ROI, VERSAILLES

With many varieties of trained fruit, the Potager du Roi is still a spectacular sight.

One of the grandest of edible gardens is the Potager du Roi (King's Kitchen Garden), created between 1678 and 1683 by Jean-Baptiste de la Quintinie for Louis XIV. The king was a keen amateur gardener and, although de la Quintinie preferred a fertile site some distance from the palace, the king wanted his royal creation to be where he could walk in it and survey the gardeners at work. And he was doing the paying. So de la Quintinie found himself draining an area known as 'The Stinking Swamps', a piece of ground of which he commented *"de la nature de celles qu'on voudrait ne trouver nulle part"* – "of a sort you would never want to find anywhere".

Good soil was imported and manured, and the 9-hectare (25-acre) garden was laid out with a large central courtyard, the Grand Carré – made up of 16 square vegetable plots, each surrounded by fruit trees – and a viewing terrace. Beyond a high surrounding wall were 29 gardens, whose microclimate enabled fruit and vegetables to be grown over an extended season.

The 5,000 trees at Versailles are trained into formal geometric forms, elaborate espaliers forming a living backbone to the vegetables, and beautiful all year round. Formative pruning was an art that de la Quintinie perfected. A key method was to hard-prune young trees to delay fruiting, in order that they fruited for a longer period and more heavily. "*Tardez vos jouissances pour jouir plus fort et plus longtemps*," he explained. Gardeners tend to be earthy, both literally and metaphorically, and royal gardeners no less so than any other sort. Bringing to mind a kind of tantric horticulture, this phrase is usually translated as "Delay your orgasms in order to climax more strongly and for a longer time."

The Potager du Roi was an enormous and intensive enterprise, but it brought great kudos and international bragging rights. Louis XIV displayed the wonders of his garden to important visitors and sent gifts of his favourite pear, Bon Chrétien, to other heads of state. Today the garden is open to the public and managed by the École Nationale Supérieure de Paysage (ENSP). It produces over 50 tonnes of fruit annually which is sold at the school and at markets in Versailles.

EUROPEAN ORCHARDS IN THE TWENTIETH CENTURY

By the end of the First World War, research into tree-fruit-growing had become more formalized. In the UK, institutes and research centres including Long Ashton, The John Innes Horticultural Institute (now the John Innes Centre) and East Malling were set up to help develop new varieties and research ways of combating pests and diseases. Then, after the Second World War, dwarfing rootstocks were widely adopted commercially. This was a major revolution. Productivity increased because the trees could be planted more closely together, and smaller trees meant that sunlight could reach a greater proportion of the fruit, so the product was more consistent. The fruit could also be efficiently picked and pruned from the ground, eliminating the need for ladders. Furthermore, trees on dwarfing rootstocks fruit at a younger age than full-sized trees, delivering quicker returns for the farmers.

Trees that are grafted on to dwarfing rootstocks will never grow to be large.

These changes fundamentally altered the way that commercial orchards operated and how they were laid out and managed. The agricultural practice became more to do with high yields – which increased by around 400 per cent – than about the use of land for a range of complementary purposes. The trees themselves came to be viewed as more of a 'crop' in the conventional agricultural sense, with a shorter life cycle

The developments of the twentieth century represented a turning point. In the 'traditional orchard' model, the land was also used in other, complementary ways. The 'modern commercial orchard' was economically a monoculture.

-35-

Traditional *Streuobst-wiesen* or meadow orchards, like this one in the Odenwald, are still occasionally found in Germany.

and lower level of sustainability, and they were replaced much more frequently. In turn, this altered the economic balance. The smaller, more traditional orchards became unviable and were neglected or grubbed up to make space for other crops. And this combination of increased orchard efficiency and the loss of the traditional model had an impact on the landscape and environment that was felt across Europe.

So, the fruit-growing developments of the twentieth century represented a turning point. The 'traditional orchard' model had trees spaced at some distance from each other, with the land also used in other, complementary ways. The 'modern commercial orchard' comprised densely packed dwarf trees, which had a much higher cropping level but the orchard was economically a monoculture. The economic benefits of the new model, coupled with government efficiency drives, spelled disaster for the traditional way.

The fortunes of British commercial orchards

In Britain, orchards and growers were hit hard by both the decline of traditional fruit-growing and by trade and economic developments. In

TRADITIONAL ORCHARDS AND AGROFORESTRY

The old-fashioned orchard often represents an agroforestry system, with tall trees interspersed with other crops and fruit bushes, or with meadow for hay or grazing. This can be seen in the Mediterranean olive grove, Spanish citrus grove or the traditional, small-scale planting of cherries and apples in France or England.

It is estimated that in the mid-twentieth century there were about 2 million hectares (approximately 5 million acres) of traditional European orchard. France had its *vergers* and *prés-vergers*; there were the German *Streuobstwiesen*, or meadow orchards, of scattered trees with grazing underneath; and other countries had similar arrangements. But the area devoted to traditional orchard has declined substantially in the last 60 years. Where trees are still associated with permanent grassland, it is usually simply grazed or mown, rather than being worked as a patchwork of crops, and this reduces the opportunity for a variety of products, income streams and activities.

the mid-twentieth century, fruit imports had been restricted in various ways, but these restrictions were gradually lifted. By the 1970s, new high-yielding varieties such as Golden Delicious and Granny Smith dominated the market but needed more warmth to ripen than is found in Britain's cool climate. Tasty local varieties still thrived but were in some cases slow-growing, lower-yielding and more pricey. Thus, growers faced greater competition, and in the latter part of the twentieth century many commercial orchards were taken out of production, and importing apples became the norm.

For some decades, things looked bad for fruit-growing in the UK. But when varieties such as Braeburn and Gala from New Zealand proved to perform well, investment and grower confidence increased. By 2009 new orchards were being planted, at modern densities of up to 3,500 trees per hectare (1,400 per acre) – as compared with fewer than 150 trees per hectare (60 per acre) in a traditional orchard. With the processes mechanized as never before, by 2011 the British market share had climbed by over 60 per cent from its lowest point.

DRINKING THE PROFITS

In Britain, many farms had small orchards for culinary fruit and for cider, and the cider was often given to labourers in lieu of pay. This practice only became illegal in 1917.

ABOVE: A heavy and early cropper, Greensleeves was introduced in 1966 and is the offspring of James Grieve and Golden Delicious.

OPPOSITE: Fundamentally practical, orchards can also be deeply romantic.

THE BIG PICTURE

Taking a bird's-eye view of the situation in Europe today, it is clear that there are several different things going on. The newer orchards are a success for the commercial fruit-growing industry, and this should be applauded in terms of the availability of local food, maintaining rural employment opportunities, and the economic viability of the farming community.

But in terms of biodiversity, heritage, conservation and farm-specific, region-specific tradition, it is not the same thing at all. These are not traditional British farm orchards, or indeed French *vergers*, German *Streuobstwiesen* or any other form of non-intensive orchard planting. Such traditional models are increasingly rare landscape features that are in need of conservation.

Cautiously, however, it could be said that the traditional, smaller-scale and less mechanized growing methods are experiencing a modern revival elsewhere – in domestic gardens, on allotments and in community orchards. New information and varieties, and the tides of fashion and economy, have reawakened widespread interest in orchard gardening. There are new possibilities for involvement and, arguably, also more opportunities than there have been for generations.

Orchard gardening and orchard farming has never been a static process. It has evolved according to personal, economic and social need, and according to the techniques, varieties and manpower available. Whether the goal is food, drink or animal fodder; whether trees are planted for subsistence or status – what people have wanted to achieve from an orchard has changed throughout history, and this is still true today.

The cloth of orchard gardening can be cut according to the needs, resources and tastes of the individual and the local community.

Allotments have seen a revival, and many permit the inclusion of small fruit trees.

And, while orchards today are picturesque and romantic, it is worth remembering that at one time they would have been a serious source of income and nutrition. Farmers would have spent less time enjoying the pretty wildlife and more time fending it off the precious crop. The chemical-spray programmes used were, at times, hair-raising, and harvest was labour-intensive and sometimes dangerous. So we must not label the whole concept 'museum piece'. Certainly, preservation in approximate stasis might work in some cases. This is, after all, a huge part of our cultural landscape, and efforts to conserve the remnants of traditional orchards should be made. But there is another, parallel way.

Conservation philosophy espouses a process of managed change, in order that, as society changes, it doesn't lose the things that create its value. So, in addition to conservation efforts, we must also embrace change in society and landscape. If you can't live with and engage with the orchards, in whatever form they take, you can't enjoy them properly. The cloth of orchard gardening can be cut according to the needs, resources and tastes of the individual and the local community. This must, surely, bestow a far greater chance of success and enjoyment on all concerned. In the next chapter we will explore this idea further.

A BRIEF HISTORY OF AMERICAN POMOLOGY

Shifting our gaze from Europe, let us take a moment to recount the enjoyable tale of intrigue that is the story of apples in North America.

When European settlers colonized America they took with them grafted trees and apple pips. Hopes were high, but for a tree originating in the congenial climate of Kent or the Loire Valley, America is a land of harsh extremes: often hotter, dryer, colder or more humid than the tree was bred for. Some places lent themselves to fruit production: the Eastern Seaboard was a decent option, while the good soil, abundant water, warm days and cool nights of Washington State is close to perfection. But elsewhere, the grafted European trees tended not to thrive.

The seedling trees were a different story, however. Not only were they genetically diverse but also they could be planted by the sackful. The results were haphazard but the physical variations prolific, and some prospered in the new environment – cheaply filling the settlers' land with food for man and beast. And, in this strange new world, even the dodgiest seedling apple must have been comforting. (On taking an ill-advised bite of an unripe persimmon, Captain John Smith of Jamestown noted that it would "draw a man's mouth awrie with much torment".)

With time, the best of these vigorous seed-grown trees were selected, propagated and conserved. As the frontiers expanded and the pioneers headed west, apples became embedded in American culture – a diverse wellspring, source of the national drink and myriad foodstuffs: the sweet juice of burstingly ripe American Summer

Roxbury Russet is believed to be the oldest cultivar bred in the USA.

Pearmain; apple butter from Swiss Limbertwig and Pumpkin Sweet; fried Northern Spy and Summer Banana.

A fall from grace

But, as in Europe, the fortunes of the orchards rose and fell, and by the 1820s an age of improvement had dawned: one of moral reform and agricultural progress. The apple trees found themselves under attack from several quarters. By this point the consumption of alcohol in America was, per capita, one of the highest in the world. While apples were food, 'new cider' or 'sweet cider' – or just cider (much to the confusion of modern Brits,

Apples are promiscuous and will cross-pollinate widely.

for whom this is clearly just apple juice) was a popular drink. Fermented, it became alcoholic, and the widely drunk 'hard cider' could be further strengthened, fortified or distilled.

In the early days, the temperance movement focused on spirits like whisky, and considered hard cider to be reasonably benign. In 1784, the social reformer Dr Benjamin Rush created a 'Moral and Physical Thermometer' to chart the progress of temperance and intemperance, writing that cider and perry produced "Cheerfulness, Strength and Nourishment, when taken only at meals, and in moderate quantities".

But, as the crusade accelerated, alcohol in every form became demonized. Pious farmers who were used to viewing the apple harvest as God's nourishing bounty found themselves castigated for harbouring a tree that was a slippery slope to moral downfall. Some reformers persuaded farmers to use apples to fatten hogs, rather than for food; the

Juice pours into the tray as the rack-and-cloth 'cheese' is compressed. Pressing apples was popular, but fermenting the drink was a slippery slope to ruin.

Fruit at Greys Court, Oxfordshire. In temperance America, apples found their name increasingly blackened. No longer were they God's easy bounty; they were a source of inevitable moral downfall.

conversion of fruit to profit oiling the argument very effectively. Others took a more fire-and-brimstone approach. In 1827, an article that was published and republished in farming and religious journals across the country answered the question that must surely have been on the lips of every Christian farmer: "What shall I do with my apples?" With impressive moral fatalism, the article made the case that apples gathered must inevitably be made into cider, which would inevitably be sold to a distiller to make brandy, "and if the brandy is sold, it must be drank, and in this way every barrel will make and circulate liquid fire enough to ruin a soul, if not destroy a life". The conclusion was that the only righteous path for the unfortunate owner of seedling apple trees was to "BURN THEM".

Although it is likely that more orchards were quietly abandoned than were actually chopped down or burned, the destruction of the apple orchards in response to the maniacal zeal of the temperance reformers remains part of the folklore of New England and the Midwest to this day.

The attack of commerce and reason

Meanwhile, the forces of a different sort of improvement were assembling against America's seedling orchards. 'Scientific' arguments proposed that trees declined with age, cropping less well and producing less robust seedlings than did newer, younger trees. The idea was that any cultivar had a finite lifespan, beyond which neither the tree nor grafts taken from it would live. The science itself didn't hold water, but it was based on observation, including the fact that older orchards were less productive and healthy than new ones. (In fact, this is more likely to be due to the accumulation of apple-specific pests and disease in established orchards. Also, if a sucker from an apple tree that had done handsomely on one site fared poorly 800km [500 miles] away, there was a tendency to attribute this to the hapless tree rather than to the difference in local conditions.)

Then the agricultural reformers turned up with Progress. In the 1820s and 1830s they repositioned apples as a commodity rather than a seasonal bonus. They also promoted grafted trees for better, more marketable crops, emphasizing the benefits of reliability and good storage in the pursuit of profit. This agricultural reform had a profound impact on the nature of America's orchards.

The golden age

The grafted cultivars generated unprecedented interest and were readily adopted. A 1905 publication by the United States Department of Agriculture entitled *Nomenclature of the Apple: A catalog of the known varieties referred to in American publications from 1804 to 1904*, lists 17,000 different apple names. Many are synonyms or possibly minor local variations, but estimates range from a conservative-but-realistic 6,500 to a whopping-but-hard-to-verify 14,000 varieties of apple in the USA by the end of the nineteenth century.

To a modern consumer with diminished palate and high aesthetic expectations, this varietal bounty must seem far in excess of need. But in the nineteenth century, apples came in every shape and size - round as a cherry or lumpy as a potato;

Rough-skinned russet apples have fallen from commercial favour.

THE TALE OF JOHNNY APPLESEED

This is a story at the core of American identity. True in origin, it has been embellished and reimagined many times. It is the myth of the ragged, barefoot-yet-saintly itinerant, bringing the blessing of fruit to pioneer families in the eighteenth century while living a life of purity and self-denial. A pomological Father Christmas, with a sack of pips on his back and a superhuman drive for planting apple trees wherever he went.

Born on the eve of the American Revolution, John Chapman just happened to live in the middle of the cultural event that was the expansion into the trans-Appalachian West in the last years of the eighteenth century. And he did indeed travel long miles, but rather than strewing pips at random, he carefully planted seedling orchards that he would tend every few years before selling them on to settlers as a means of sustaining their families.

Beyond the dreamy, sepia-toned beneficence there are many stories: the eccentric apple-tree planter was vegetarian, celibate, preacher; a follower of theologian Emmanuel Swedenborg. It is said that his preference for wild apple trees stemmed from a religious objection to grafting and that he attached a symbolic importance to wild apples. Some welcomed him; others found him strange. There was much to fuel a lively story.

Towards the end of his career, the cultural landscape and agricultural practices were changing. But the poetry of Johnny Appleseed – a man singularly dedicated to bringing his fruit trees to the people – remains to this day. To read more, see *Johnny Appleseed and the American Orchard* by William Kerrigan, listed in Resources.

glossy, matt, waxy or sandpaper-rough; hard, low-sugar varieties that would last into winter and soft, sweet ones that would explode when they fell. There was an apple for every purpose – a pantheon of spots, stripes, flushes, streaks and russetting. And, while the Atlantic coast and parts of the Midwest saw extraordinary diversity, there were even apples that adapted to grow in the hot Deep South.

But, as in Europe, the drive for efficiency, advances in refrigerated storage and cheap railway transport sounded the death knell for quirky heritage varieties. Soft drinks competed with the traditional American cider (apple juice). Enterprises focused on growing massive numbers of fewer fruit types. This brought 14,000 varieties down to the 100 or so that are commercially grown today, and simplified consumer choice to three easy colour-coded options: for much of the twentieth century, Red Delicious, Golden Delicious and (green) Granny Smith reigned supreme.

There is an old saying: 'If you plant pears, you plant for your heirs.' The oldest documented living fruit trees are both pears: one believed to have been planted in Cape Town, in the Dutch East India Company's garden, in 1656; the other planted by John Endecott, the first Governor of the Massachusetts Bay Colony in Danvers, between 1630 and 1632.

BARRIE JUNIPER

The long and illustrious career of Barrie Juniper – botanist, geneticist, and Emeritus Fellow of St Catherine's College, Oxford – had many highlights. But when it came to fruit, one truly significant discovery waited until he had retired.

"*I had created a living DNA apple library at Wytham, near Oxford, with old apples such as Shakespeare's Leathercoat and new apples like Sunset; French apples such as Orleans Reinette, the cider apple Tom Putt, and a hundred more. I was keen to thrash out what they had, or did not have, in common, and where they might have originated,*" says Barrie.

Pioneering work by the Soviet scientist Nikolai Vavilov, recovered after the Cold War, revealed that, before his death in prison in 1943, he had pointed to the Tien Shan as the possible origin of at least one parent of the domesticated apple.

New access to the ex-Soviet Republics now presented Barrie with an unmissable opportunity to seek out the DNA of real wild apples. He returned from the mountains between China and Uzbekistan with samples of apple leaves for genetic sequencing.

"*At the time, the 'sweet' apple was always written as Malus x domestica, the 'x' indicating that it was a hybrid of some sort. But the parents were unknown,*" says Barrie. "*We had looked at every domestic apple we could and found no evidence of any hybridity at all, meaning that the sweet apple is, unlike most crops, a complete sexual snob.*"

Barrie's research led to the publication, with David Mabberley, of *The Story of the Apple* (2006), which argued that, rather than arising from human hybridizing of local varieties, apples all came from somewhere else entirely. But exactly how ("*mostly inside a horse*") and when ("*probably pre-Roman*") remains in dispute.

And from this came an extensive varietal range. "*Head gardeners and fruit breeders were always searching for patronage. 'Would his Lordship or her Ladyship like a brand new variety to be named after him or her?' 'Yes, please!' said the Duke of Devonshire, Lord Lambourne, Lady Sudeley, and so on. Such nomenclature added to the market potential and did the head gardener's Christmas bonus no harm either!*" smiles Barrie.

"*But don't think for a minute that apples are 'English'. They are Eurasian. They are much, much older than generations of horticulturists realized, and their real Latin name should be Malus pumila!*"

CHAPTER TWO

AN ORCHARD TAPESTRY

Our landscapes contain an enormous number of fruit trees. In towns, cities and in the wider countryside, solitary specimens and small clusters abound. Sometimes, these can form a productive continuum – sprawls of diverse and productive trees, around and within areas of human habitation – which represent, to all intents and purposes, an informal and invisible orchard.

In the UK, the 'traditional orchard' has been clearly defined for conservation purposes, as described opposite. But this definition can also be employed in a different and parallel way. What happens if we apply the same concept to our immediate environment? If we extrapolate the notion of orchard to cover the domestic landscape?

This chapter explores this idea, while also taking a look at trees that, although perhaps not originally part of a commercial or domestic orchard, are nevertheless fruiting, supporting wildlife and contributing to the local scene. It considers the role of the orchard in the community and landscape as it now exists and as we now inhabit it, taking a look at the places where orchards used to grow and where relict orchards or orchard fragments remain. And, while urban orchards are increasingly celebrated, there are also places where tree fruit grows unplanned and unnoticed.

Even in city centres there can be a productive continuum of semi-adjacent fruit trees.

TRADITIONAL AND RELICT ORCHARDS

Here, orchard definitions are discussed from a British perspective, but there are many parallel stories elsewhere. Increasingly, orchard conservationists and enthusiasts in different countries communicate, exchange and explore ideas. Groups are often led by a range of organizations with a mutual goal, or have a reciprocal international remit. As individuals and nations we are connected globally, so, as interest reawakens, it makes sense to look across borders and oceans for inspiration that can be adopted in our own backyards.

Defining an orchard

A traditional orchard is defined by the People's Trust for Endangered Species (PTES) and Natural England as "groups of fruit and nut trees planted on vigorous rootstocks at low densities in permanent grassland, and managed in a low-intensity way". The minimum size of the orchard is five trees, with crown edges less than 20m (66') apart.

This definition may appear strict or even arbitrary, but it is a useful tool in identifying orchards as priority habitat. It demarcates the site and allocates boundaries. Although the situation is fluid – trees may grow, age or die, and the use of the surrounding landscape may evolve – it means that the status of any orchard can be assessed at any point in time. It also characterizes an orchard for surveying purposes, enabling

Orchard fragments and relict trees can easily disappear into the undergrowth.

A relict orchard has fewer than five trees.

'ground-truthing'. This is where volunteer surveyors verify the status of sites to generate 'real' data that will help to refine maps and implement conservation measures.

By its very nature, the above definition is conservative – in the sense of being about conservation. It allows orchard restoration projects to protect sites for future generations, and it highlights orchards' biodiversity, cultural and heritage value. But this is an inherently retrospective viewpoint: it considers an orchard's current status as a product of its former status. It doesn't consider its future status as a product of its current status (other than in the simplest sense of 'preserved to be enjoyed'). It does not (and is not supposed to) look forward to how an individual might embrace an orchard in the broadest interpretation of the word. This is an important distinction.

Marginal sites and other types of orchard

The designation of 'marginal sites' aims to classify orchard growth that does not fall within such a strict definition. A relict orchard, for example, is a site with fewer than five trees or where the trees are spread too widely apart. This term is usually applied to fragments of what was once a much larger orchard, and can even refer to a single old tree.

In addition, there are other permutations of status and management, including 'long abandoned', 'intensively managed traditional orchard' and 'abandoned or organic bush orchard'.

LANDSCAPE OLD AND NEW

From this definition of a 'traditional' orchard, it is clear that we are talking about very low-density planting. To stand in a cluster of trees that conforms to this model would potentially not feel crowded. Less like standing in a wood; more like parkland. And there would be a lot more going on than just trees. The question is, is there so much going on in our inhabited landscapes that we can't see the trees at all?

The old orchard at Grim's Dyke in Harrow Weald is being restored and replanted.

Historically, orchards would often have been planted on rural farms and around large conurbations. Populations need to be fed, and the closer the source of food, the lower the costs and the less chance it has to deteriorate before it is consumed. Larger gardens too would have had orchards, both for pleasure and to feed the household, while abbeys and monasteries also cultivated and processed large quantities of fruit.

Yet as populations grew and cities expanded, some of these orchards on the outskirts of town were built upon. And, while they must regularly have been razed to the ground, in some cases the spacing of both trees and houses would have meant that there was no practical need to cut down all the trees. Saving himself a job, a Victorian builder might leave the remaining trees between the rows of houses as 'mature garden planting', a veritable asset. A scattering of mature trees might be incorporated into the street scene, or left as fragments of parkland and green.

In the countryside beyond the sprawling suburbs, it was twentieth-century agricultural intensification that sounded the death knell for old-style orchards. Many were grubbed up and others became neglected – grown through with opportunistic competitors to create mixed woodland, or left gradually decaying in fields as uncared-for clusters of wizened trees. Decades later, any remaining fruit trees might be screened by surrounding woodland, or simply grown so far from cultivation that they are unrecognizable: old, gnarled and too meagre to impress themselves on the passer-by.

NEWBURY LOCK

At Newbury in Berkshire, the Kennet and Avon Canal and the River Kennet form a network of waterways: they meet and part, join and divide, step down through locks and tumble over weirs.

Near the high street, Lock Island is a spit of land sandwiched between the river and the canal. From about 1720 until it was damaged by fire

The garden by Newbury Lock is hung with fruit trees.

in 1989, this attractive spot was the site of the lock-keeper's cottage. Although the last lock-keeper retired in1958, this is a place that has been lived in and gardened for centuries. Local records indicate that land nearby was used for agriculture and horticulture in the 1300s, and several culti-vated apple trees remain on the main part of the island next to the footpath.

On the other side of the lock, there is another story. A precipitous fragment of land is bisected by a gated brick wall leading to a tiny space that once was part of the garden of the seventeenth-century Old Globe Inn. Tended by local hero and canal-saviour John Gould until his death, this minute orchard island is hung with old apple and pear trees, heavy with fruit and guarded by water.

Apple trees blossom in central Newbury.

Is There an Orchard Near Me?

Various groups can provide details of where orchards can be found and where they used to be. The list below is a starting point. For full contact details and websites, see Resources.

Organizations and online resources

✻ The People's Trust for Endangered Species (PTES) in England and Wales has identified traditional orchard sites from aerial photographs, marking locations on an interactive map on its website. The website also has a useful 'FruitFinder' database. Contact PTES for a survey pack with instructions, a map of orchards in your area and identification guides.

✻ The Urban Orchard Project is an orchard scheme that started in London before expanding to other UK cities. It is compiling a map of existing and new orchards, and likes people to get involved.

✻ The Orange Pippin orchards directory is a diverse international resource, covering regions and countries from America and Hawaii to Europe and India. Not all are traditional orchards, but many are open to the public and are managed by experts and enthusiasts. This gives an interesting snapshot of what will grow where.

✻ PickYourOwn.org is a slightly haphazard international resource, but it has an extensive list of places you can go to pick fruit of all persuasions.

✻ A swift search online using terms including your county or a specific place, fruit of choice, and 'orchard', 'traditional', 'old', etc. can reveal a wealth of information.

Maps and local societies

Orchards may be marked on current Ordnance Survey maps, and also on older maps – try the local library or museum, or search online. History societies can be a mine of information. Local historical documents and archaeological records can provide a timeline of significant events, including land use, going back even thousands of years.

Community

Ask your neighbours. Older members of a community and those whose families have lived in the area for several generations are often well informed about local history and how the area has developed over the years.

TREES IN TOWNS: FINDING THE OLD

It is important to recognize that the contemporary urban landscape has grown up from, and over, what went before. The familiar streets and the houses we live in cut across an earlier version. Our concept of permanence is in fact just the vision of a modernist of 150 years ago, profiting from the fashionable suburbs and workmen's cottages of the day. Or, indeed, the modernist of 5 years ago, striving to cram more housing units into less space. But the critical thing is that the houses around us have been built on *something:* farmland, garden or, sometimes, orchard. And these places once had trees – some of which are still here.

Where the sites of larger traditional orchards have been repurposed, the scattering of remaining trees can cross new boundaries of ownership and use. There might be a few in the grounds of a modern hospital, several in nearby gardens, and an old specimen tree in the park beyond the houses.

As late winter segues into early spring, the cherry-plum blossom floats above the Kennet and Avon Canal.

The contemporary urban landscape has grown up from, and over, what went before. The houses around us have been built on *something*: farmland, garden or, sometimes, orchard. These places once had trees, and some are still here.

Fruit hanging over garden walls is a familiar sight along our highways and byways.

The moment you start looking for tree fruit, miraculously it becomes visible. Suddenly there is an old, contorted tree; another is perhaps growing robustly, lushly productive and hidden in plain view. It is quite common to find clusters of trees on allotments, along the hedge of the parking area or next to the central track. These don't 'officially' belong to anyone and may find themselves ignored: an irony of rotting and crushed fruit amongst an otherwise cherished harvest.

On old Ordnance Survey maps of late Victorian London there are very dense concentrations of orchards to the west, in Richmond, Brentford and Twickenham – now swanky residential areas. West Fields in the Home Counties market town of Newbury is made up of a few roads that punched straight through the site of an orchard in the 1870s. And houses outside Wokingham were erected on fruit-growing land in 1910. It stands to reason that the larger the spaces between the houses,

the greater the chance that old trees will survive, and at the end of the long gardens in this Wokingham road are several venerable apple trees. They have been cut and hacked, and are creaking towards the end of their lives, but their very existence hints at a landscape past.

Fruit trees are often part of the streetscape. Here, a fig helps to soften the lines of the concrete jungle.

LONE TREES

In Britain, productive fruit trees are quite a common sight in urban parks and public gardens. These walnuts, mulberries, crab apples and almonds were never part of an orchard, but pull their weight as horticultural specimen trees. And whether they were designed into the original planting scheme, planted as a memorial or have arrived fortuitously, they mature into their townscape over time.

Peaches are certainly attractive, and it is hard to believe they could be a nuisance!

The story of traditional orchards

becoming neglected, built upon or overgrown is repeated in many countries. In some regions, cities gradually expand into agricultural land. Elsewhere, rural farms are abandoned as people move to the cities for work. In Spain, citrus, grape, pomegranate and fig trees can be seen surviving among ruins, when other signs of cultivation are long gone.

America's tree-fruit fortunes have fluctuated in the face of politics and progress. Today, in a country that is one of the biggest apple producers in the world and which has created some of the most globally successful apple 'brands', the apple is the nation's signature fruit. But, as in Europe, smaller orchards have been outcompeted by vast fruit-producing monsters and the regional and local palimpsest of flavour has been eroded.

But when the contemporary streetscapes of Britain and the United States are compared, there are key differences in culture and legal framework. While the roads of Britain are lined with feral apples and the streets of some European towns with dates or oranges, fruit is not sanctioned for planting in cities in most American states, under the doctrine of 'attractive nuisance' – effectively banning fruit on public land.

But this status quo is being challenged, and change is afoot with energetic and progressive urban orchard movements. The Los-Angeles-based Fallen Fruit has been publishing maps for years, taking advantage of another old law that renders fruit hanging over the sidewalk as public property, and they have just opened a 'radical' public fruit garden. There are equally vigorous movements in other cities, including The Boston Tree Party and the Philadelphia Orchard Project.

Awareness of issues surrounding the conservation of regional orchard heritage is on the increase, and some people are also taking access into their own hands – like the Guerrilla Grafters of San Francisco Bay, who surreptitiously graft fruit-bearing branches on to non-fruiting trees, as a free public food resource.

As in residential areas, handsome trees in public places may be remnants of earlier gardens – particularly on sites that were defensive or ecclesiastical. Universities, schools, the Church and large businesses often acquire substantial historic buildings, and their surrounding green space, for their activities, and any surviving fruiting trees become a pleasant social serendipity.

Mulberries are positively common as urban trees. Bristol is quietly littered with them, in the Royal Fort Gardens, in Portland Square and in Victoria Square. There is one outside Exeter Cathedral and another in the Abbots Garden at Tintern Abbey, and they appear frequently in the gardens of Oxford and Cambridge colleges.

Walnuts and sweet chestnuts also fall into the handsome amenity tree category. There are vast sweet chestnuts in various places in the British

Mulberry trees are fairly common in towns and cities.

Isles (the biggest, found near St Leonard's Church in Tortworth, Gloucestershire, is probably nearly 1,000 years old), but respectably mature chestnuts can also be found in London's Royal Parks, around school playing fields and in university grounds. They are perhaps less common in North America, although Kits Beach in Vancouver boasts a fruiting specimen, but there are always discoveries to be made in the most familiar of urban landscapes.

ULTRA-URBAN ORCHARDS

In twenty-first-century cities, something new and exciting is happening. The zeitgeist is sustainable living, and orchards are being brought back to town: old ones restored, new ones planted, and community fruit schemes initiated.

This fruity fervour has gripped everyone, from architects to evangelists; ecologists to artists. Community groups and local councils are, on this occasion, heading in the same direction. In the UK, The Urban Orchard Project declares that it is "dedicated to creating inspiring cities swathed in trees, providing beautiful blossom and tasty fruit, everywhere", while the Philadelphia Orchard Project is engaged in a similar mission.

The Perth Cultural Centre in Western Australia has a community orchard garden and, overlooking the River Thames in London, the Queen Elizabeth Roof Garden at the Southbank Centre has orchard trees underplanted with wildflowers and vegetables. People can enjoy contact with productive nature at a level that suits them: with a cup of coffee and a paper, picking fruit from a tree, or brandishing a jam pan in the kitchen.

Almost without exception, these projects are about local food and conservation at some level, with a real focus on gaining skills and improving the lives of local people. Shared from group to group and from country to country is an increasingly robust bank of information and support

ABOVE: A walnut thrives in the car park of a Berkshire Baptist church. This specimen would be dwarfed by the black walnut in Castle Park in Sered', Slovakia: the largest in Europe. It is estimated to be 300 years old and is 25m (82') high, with a 6.3m (21') circumference.

OPPOSITE: Quince is an underused specimen tree. Popular in Europe, it is less common in the American kitchen, although it can be found growing ornamentally in the cloister at Fort Tryon Park in Manhattan.

At the Queen Elizabeth Roof Garden in London, orchards of apples and olives are enjoyed.

for would-be urban orchardists. There are humble homespun community gardens and modest permaculture projects; inner-city fruit forests, participatory planting schemes and great juggernauts of social change and urban agriculture. But, whatever the scale, the message is clear and consistent: that a connection to food production and the natural world is valued and desired; that it is something healthy and inspiring – a valuable social adhesive. It seems that the urban orchard movement is here to stay.

THE ACCIDENTAL ORCHARD

City centres favour those species with a foot in both ornamental and productive camps, as we have seen. But with parks managed for intensive leisure use, the opportunity for spontaneous fruit in an unkempt hedgerow, semi-permanent scrub or borders gone feral is reduced. Yet you don't have to go very far from the centre of town for anti-establishment undergrowth to take advantage of the slightly scruffier sort of urban park and pathway.

And, beyond the straight lines and shrubberies of town, the fields, hedges and waysides are sprinkled liberally with fruit trees. Some may be the result of horticultural endeavour, but most are the truly wild fruit that seeds itself in the hedgerows, and 'wildings' that have sprung up from discarded apple cores and plum stones.

Fruit in the wild

Nature is generous. Hedgerows rapidly fill up with blackberries, damsons and cherries. And, while the rural wayside is the spiritual home of wild fruit, urban lanes too can be woolly with blackthorn, yielding sloes aplenty, and cherries leaning drunkenly from copses and boundaries.

Frothy in spring, blackthorn yields an autumn harvest of sloes.

Wherever people have been, there is a legacy of lunches past. Bomb sites, industrial estates, airfields and sites of former factories can yield the harvest of a long-ago pip: rich pickings for the modern forager. Along railway lines and towpaths; around car parks, along roadsides and in the lean, unkempt growth that surrounds allotment sites and recreation grounds, there will be fruit: wild, feral and haphazard.

In well-travelled places, this fruit takes little finding. Decades of munching motorists, gaily slinging their cores out of the window, has resulted in highways that are lined with an abstract fruit forest. The UK road and motorway network is positively laden. If you leave the M4 at any junction in Berkshire, the autumn roadside is bright with golden-yellow apples. And, at the right time of year, the A4 near Reading and the M5 in Gloucestershire can be an almost continuous hedge of fruit. It would be the height of foolishness to harvest alongside a fast road, but there is fun to be had in playing spot-the-apple.

But there is no need to take a pilgrimage to the west of England in search of a fruit fix. There will be something similar and regionally appropriate in every neighbourhood, town and country. Wildings and wild fruit will grow where they find themselves. If we take a proper look at the scenery, it can feed and delight us.

Cultivated hedges

Hedges are common, even ubiquitous, in Britain, but they also appear in Europe, the United States and beyond, as either man-made or sponta-neous features. Comprising a multitude of woody species and growing more complex with time, they often yield incidental harvests of wild cherries, sloes, hazelnuts and elderberries, as well as the borderline-edible crab apple and wild pear species. But, in addition to the sponta-neous native fruit of the region, there is a tradition of augmenting

THE CHRISTMAS PIPPIN

While many new apples are carefully bred, there are still some that are discovered in the old-fashioned way. The sweet and aromatic Christmas Pippin was spotted as a roadside seedling on the M5 in Somerset in 2005 by retired horticulturist Geoffrey Rowson. One can just imagine the fruit enthusiast, captivated by the sight of the laden tree, ducking and diving through the back roads to find it. Screeching to a halt and leaping out to swipe a handful of apples, taste buds alive.

In most cases, there the story would have ended. But in the case of the Christmas Pippin the apple was exceptional and the finder well informed. Geoffrey Rowson sent the fruit to several industry contacts. They approved. A mission was mounted to collect wood for grafting and the tree was successfully propagated, and by 2011 the chance pip had become a commercially available variety.

Read the full story at Fruit Forum (see Resources).

hedgerows with useful species. In Britain, *Prunus insititia* variants such as damsons, mirabelles and purple or golden bullaces, for example, are frequently found.

Resourceful medieval farmers would plant orchard trees in hedgerows and on headlands. This is a practice which, according to Richard Mabey's *Flora Britannica*, has persisted in Lincolnshire, with hedges containing apples, plums, pears and, more surprisingly, rhubarb. There are wilding pears in hedges in the Vale of the White Horse in Oxfordshire, and crab apples were the third-most-mentioned boundary species in Anglo-Saxon and Welsh charters.

In Cumbria, hedges enclosing fields or smallholdings would be planted with one crab apple or wilding to every three thorn bushes, resulting in an immensely diverse – although now aged – fruit-filled hedgerow. Mabey also recounts the tale of an old countryman in Evesham in the

ABOVE LEFT: It is common practice for thrifty farmers to augment their hedges with edible trees.

ABOVE RIGHT: Wild damsons spill out of a Welsh hedgerow.

1940s who would walk around with a pocket full of domestic apple cuttings. When he came across a suitable crab apple he would graft a 'proper' apple to it, resulting in a high proportion of cultivated apples in the local hedges and a pleasant surprise for passers-by.

What to look for

Genuinely wild fruit stretches out along rural hedgerows, added to by human hand and augmented by the bastard offspring of cultivated fruit – random hybrids of indeterminate origin. But the best place to look for trees is in the abstract fruit salad of historical human activity – where people have lived in the past or still do – and the more people the better.

By the middle of summer, the chances of finding fruit dangling over walls and fences, bursting out of hedges or bravely ripening at the edge of car parks is high. The bounty begins with stone fruit such as cherry plums (*Prunus cerasifera*) and bird cherries (*Prunus avium*), and moves on to mulberries and damsons, pears and apples, and the sloes that take the harvest through to mid-autumn and beyond. But one of the challenges of harvesting wild fruit is not so much spotting it in the first place but actually managing to be there, with a bag, when it is ripe. So it is worth identifying likely candidates well in advance.

All sorts of goodies lurk beyond the cultivated pale, but self-sown trees don't present themselves in neat and identifiable varieties. This is fruit in the raw – a long way from the homogeneity of the supermarket and the neat mini-trees of modern commercial orchards. These trees are unkempt and tangled; wild men of the woods who have never felt the touch of a pair of loppers. They are gnarled and untidy, growing regardless of human activity as well as because of it. And in some cases they are hanging on by their toes.

In the winter-black hedgerow it takes practice to distinguish the lurking prize, but, come spring, there is a gay eruption of blossom as the trees put out their pink and white flags. Older and more neglected trees may not produce much fruit, but the existence of blossom is a good start. Some trees – figs, walnuts, hazels and elderberries – are clearly identifiable at this point, while blossom from the plum, apple and pear families are all distinctively different. Flowers may give no indication as to the size, flavour or quantity of the eventual fruit, but you can narrow down whether it is, for example, a cherry or a pear.

As the season goes on, more clues emerge as to the identity of each mystery tree. It is perhaps not a crab apple but a culinary apple; the green polka dots on the 'sort of plum tree' brighten to red and orange,

ABOVE LEFT:
Damson blossom has delicate, translucent white petals.

ABOVE RIGHT:
Cherries bear flowers and fruit on long stems.

The plum reveals its true colours as it ripens.

revealing it to be a cherry plum rather than a damson. As the trees become familiar, a conscious connection emerges – a delightful personal secret between you and the landscape. Wayside edibles peep through the familiar undergrowth, sharp, aromatic and fresh. While the fabric of county or country may vary, the edible landscape endures.

THE PATCHWORK ORCHARD

Another type of accidental or invisible orchard can be found closer to home. Looking out of my bathroom window on to my suburban garden, I come eye-to-eye with a cooking apple. To its immediate right is a pear. Another apple, possibly Blenheim Orange, is at the far end of the garden, and to the front is a crab apple. Overlooking, for the moment, the fact that I also have an apple, a pear, two peach trees, a cherry and a Szechuan pepper in containers, that is already four fruit trees within the curtilage of my house. Applying the five-trees rule, that is practically an orchard.

But if I look to my right (still out of the bathroom window) there is an old cherry tree next door. And to the left, my nearest neighbour has an old apple, a columnar apple, a pear and a bush cooking apple. The neighbour beyond that has a standard apple, an espalier and a fig. Beyond that, there is a laden pear tree, with a large walnut in the distance. More I cannot see.

All the neighbouring gardens are about the same size as mine, and in just five houses, or an area of about 20m by 40m (66' by 132'), there are at least 13 trees – or 19 if you count my containers. Make that 20 if you count the walnut, some 50m (165') from my window, but a small hop from my neighbours. And, myself excluded, this is not a street of plant nuts or orchard fanatics – these are the ordinary gardens owned by people with day jobs and an average level of interest in horticulture.

MESSAGE FROM BEYOND THE GRAVE

The Fig Tree Tomb in St Mary's Church, Watford is said to be the grave of an atheist who asked to be buried with a fig in their hand, declaring that if there was an afterlife the fig would sprout. The existence of God was proven when a fig tree emerged, dislodging the tomb lid and becoming a popular Victorian tourist attraction.

A fat and potentially juicy fig.

WILD FIGS

Despite their Mediterranean associations, figs grow rather well in Britain, although the 'wild' ones are often associated with roads, railways or industry – warm microclimates that probably aid germination.

Many, such as the Dalmarnock Fig, which grows on the banks of the River Clyde in Glasgow, are found close to sewage works – the likely source of the original seed. The largest colony in the UK is in Sheffield in the old industrial area. The theory is that in the 1920s the local steelworks used river water as a coolant, which meant that the river ran at a constant temperature of about 20°C (68°F) – warm enough for fig seeds flushed out in sewage to thrive. These trees are now seen as part of the industrial heritage of the area, and some have had Tree Preservation Orders placed upon them.

Figs thrive in a warm microclimate, as against this wall.

The sun rises over a patchwork orchard.

And it is not just this neighbourhood. A quick survey of friends and family shows that in central Bristol, a small garden of three small fruit trees is joined by at least ten more within a 20m (66') radius. At the end of that road, the churchyard and old rectory are also planted with fruit. Elsewhere in the same city, a slightly larger garden also has three fruit trees with "several more over the back".

A similar sweep of a street near Reading University tallied fifteen: "We have three apples and one nectarine. And within a 20m radius there is one morello cherry, an old apple, three younger ones, a pear, a plum, next door's apple hedge and a walnut over the road." Meanwhile, a tiny courtyard in Highgate, London has a full orchard complement of columnar and espalier trees. Once again, in every case, the owner's interest in gardening is casual.

Now, I am quite prepared to admit that such a high local level of tree fruit may not exist in every urban road. My short survey does not take into consideration high-rise living – although even apartment blocks are rooted in the earth. As a piece of research it is unscientific and frankly full of holes: a self-selecting cohort, the geographical range of

'Orchards' of trees may exist at a greater density and frequency than we realize, sprawling out over neighbourhoods. There are the artificial boundaries of property and highway, but as the bee flies and the wind blows, is this not an orchard?

my home-owning acquaintances and the fact that I asked people who I knew had some trees to start with. But even if each of the gardens concerned contained just one tree, the criteria for the area constituting an orchard would be fulfilled by dint of the trees in adjacent gardens.

The point is that 'orchards' of trees may exist at both a greater density and frequency than is usually realized, crossing domestic boundaries and sprawling out over neighbourhoods in a higgledy-piggledy hotch-potch of accidental productivity. To be sure, this is not a 'traditional' orchard as we might imagine it. It is not made up of tall and angular standards in a country setting, grazed by pigs or sheep beneath.

But in the contemporary context, where people care for relatively small gardens and their trees are underplanted with flowers and herbs, with perhaps a pond, a patio or a few vegetables – surely this is just the latest iteration of the mixed-use purpose that traditional orchards have always had. The local human population is greater. There are the artificial boundaries of property and highway. But as the bee flies and the wind blows, is this not an orchard?

Traditional orchards are often grazed by sheep or geese.

In urban gardens, fruit trees feature among flowers and seating.

For much-garlanded orchard expert Joan Morgan, the pursuit of the story of fruit, in all its nuanced and scintillating detail, has been the odyssey of a lifetime.

When Joan was a child in the Vale of Glamorgan, each farm had a small orchard, with numerous varieties for food and cider. But later, while working in London as a research biochemist, she gradually noticed varieties disappearing. *"I remember thinking 'Where are the James Grieve and Ellison's Orange that used to be in the shops?'"*

Her career turned towards science- and garden-writing, yet this compelling question remained. She took her quest into the peerless orchards at RHS Wisley and the National Fruit Collection, delving deeper into detail as her curiosity grew.

"Flavour and history were a driving force from the outset," she explains. The quiet heroes of fruit-breeding, and those who had so lyrically and thoroughly catalogued what are now historic varieties, had particular thrall. *"My heroes in the fruit world are the nineteenth-century authority Dr Robert Hogg and his successor Edward Bunyard. I consider myself a mere apprentice by comparison!"*

This 'apprentice' ably followed in the masters' footsteps and, with Alison Richards, published *The Book of Apples* (revised as *The New Book of Apples* in 2002), which provides historical and botanical information on 2,000 varieties.

The Book of Pears followed in 2015. *"Pears was in many ways the more challenging project. It took years to compile the tasting notes for each variety and to trace their stories,"* Joan says. *"Like all fruits, pears were prized as a fashionable status symbol, and I wanted to see how far back one could go. I went to Syria and Iran, where pears were cultivated by the ancient kings. And I visited California, the world's leading producer of pears in the 1920s and 1930s."*

For her work as a fruit historian and pomologist, Joan has been awarded the RHS's Veitch Memorial Medal, the Institute of Horticulture's Outstanding Services award, and the Derek Cooper Outstanding Achievement Award 2016 at the BBC Radio 4 Food and Farming Awards.

"There is more supermarket shelf space devoted to crisps than to apples and pears!" Joan declares. *"But fruit is gorgeous, and people are increasingly realizing its value."*

CHAPTER THREE

CONSERVATION AND BIODIVERSITY

While their fortunes may have fluctuated, our trees and orchards remain culturally and environmentally significant. A traditional orchard is an ecosystem of remarkable biodiversity, and provides a refuge for numerous species, some of which are found almost nowhere else. Meanwhile, the unkempt trees of our landscape represent a genetic goldmine: a potential hoard of robust new commercial varieties.

This chapter discusses conservation of old orchards and takes a look at the plants and animals that rely on them, considering not only individual species but also the interdependent nature of elements within an ecosystem. It goes on to look at the genetic diversity of the trees themselves, which is important both for the conservation of wild fruit forests and heritage orchards, and for the purpose of breeding resilient varieties for the future.

ORCHARD CONSERVATION

As we saw in Chapter 1, traditional UK and European orchard habitat is under serious threat. Modern commercial systems produce plenty of fruit, but they support significantly less wildlife and are a much less permanent landscape feature than their predecessors. Of the traditional orchards that still exist, some are in good heart, but those that were left to their own devices over half a century ago have seen their once-rich habitat erode. Often, they are at their last gasp.

While each cluster of trees in a traditional orchard (or what's left of one) may represent a species-rich unit of habitat, it is often isolated – an island of biodiversity in less rich surroundings. With no younger trees, there is nothing to take over from the veterans as they age and die. And when the habitat becomes too diminished to support the dependent species, there is often no comparable site nearby to which they can move.

OPPOSITE: An isolated orchard of old trees may represent an island of biodiversity.

BELOW: The orchard at Canons Ashby in Northamptonshire has trees of varying ages. The grass is cut late in the season, once the flowers have seeded and the bulbs gone over.

The restored orchard at Bethlem Royal Hospital in London (see page 83).

The UK Biodiversity Action Plan (BAP) was published in 1994, as the British Government's response to the Convention on Biological Diversity held in Rio in 1992. The BAP, which describes the biological resources of the UK and provides detailed plans for their conservation, includes traditional orchards in its list of priority habitat, and this allows attempts to conserve them to be focused within a defined framework.

In recent years there has been a proliferation of conservation efforts, strategies and organizations explicitly interested in orchards. There is renewed focus on traditional methods of orchard management and on locally grown or heritage fruit, and planting new orchards and restoring old ones, particularly in urban areas and villages, has become popular.

Thus, orchards are increasingly being reclaimed by communities and used in new ways. Not only are they a social resource, but as an archetype of sustainable agriculture there is also potential for enterprise, skills acquisition and learning activities – all on the back of biodiversity.

A MANY-LAYERED WORLD

Traditional orchards are made up of a number of different elements. The 'perfect' site, in the sense of richest biodiversity, would have older trees and newer ones; standing deadwood and rotten stumps. It would have a grassland floor with a range of wildflowers and other plants, and perhaps some scrubby infill. There might be hedgerow boundaries, or adjacent ponds and streams.

Different sites will support different species. An open aspect and nectar-rich meadow will attract butterflies and moths. Abundant hedgerows and deadwood encourages beetles, while a moister spot with a dense canopy favours mosses, lichens, ferns and amphibians like frogs and newts. The flora and fauna varies according to soil type and local climate, and the species supported by cider orchards, cobnut plats, cherry fields and olive groves will inevitably be different. But what all traditional orchards have in common is that they have existed for a considerable period of time, their overall stability allowing complexity and niche habitats to develop, in which other plants and animals can live.

For an orchard to be undisturbed is not at all the same thing as being static. An orchard is a dynamic environment, and over time there will be flux. The seasons roll on. Trees mature, age and die. Grass grows long and is grazed short, and hedges are managed. Clearings arise and are filled. While the orchard may have occupied the same piece of land for centuries, the profile of tree species may have evolved according to local conditions and social need.

Wildlife can shelter among lush grass and buttercups.

For maximum biodiversity, an orchard should contain trees at all stages: from newly planted to mature, and also those in decline.

But what all traditional orchards have in common is that they have existed for a considerable period of time, their overall stability allowing complexity and niche habitats to develop, in which other plants and animals can live.

A slow pace of change means that although resources such as food and breeding sites may wax and wane, they never vanish entirely. A survey at any point in time is therefore a snapshot, predominantly featuring those organisms that are best served by the current habitat composition.

For conservation purposes and for maximum species diversity, an orchard should not only be well established, with trees of different ages, but should also exist within a network of similar orchards in the adjacent landscape. Practically, this means that a traditional orchard site should be lightly managed and regularly replenished with new trees, and that it should be considered in the context of its broader environment, as healthy orchards are not islands. Communication channels – essentially wildlife corridors – between units of biodiversity are very important.

BETHLEM ROYAL HOSPITAL, LONDON

Bethlem was founded in London in 1247, as a priory dedicated to St Mary of Bethlehem, and became the world's first psychiatric hospital in 1403. Restoration of the 90-year-old orchards began in 2010 in order to engage patients with therapeutic outdoor activities, help them develop new skills and improve mental well-being.

The Occupational Therapy Department engaged experts from The Urban Orchard Project to help identify surviving trees, source heritage varieties and organize pruning and restoration workshops. It was a great success, and apples are now used in therapeutic cooking groups, pressed for juice and dried for sale in the hospital shop. Meanwhile, a waymarked Traditional Orchards Nature Trail allows the public to explore the restored orchards and learn about the patients' work, helping to break down barriers about psychiatric care.

Slow-growing lichens are a symbiosis between fungi and algae, and are a good indicator of air quality. The most sensitive are the leafy, hairy foliose lichens, while the flatter, drier crustose lichens are more tolerant of pollution.

WILDLIFE IN THE ORCHARD

A healthy orchard provides a complex mosaic of habitats. The trees, in various states of growth or decay, together with grassland, hedges and other elements, support a range of wildlife at different stages and at different times of year.

Mosses, ferns and lichens

Veteran trees carry a huge number of passengers, including plants and lichens. These harmless epiphytes establish on the surface of the bark and can be an interesting element of orchard botany.

In areas where the air is clean and there is high atmospheric moisture, branches rapidly become shaggy. The orchard floor, too, can build up a population of mosses, ferns and lichens, growing among grasses or on exposed rocks. Lichens in particular are specific about the minerals they need and the pH of their substrate, so the greater the diversity of surfaces, the greater the diversity of things that will live on them.

Fungi

Fungi are the hidden heroes in the ecosystem, living in, on and alongside both living and dead trees. These are the decomposers and recyclers that make nutrients available for plant growth. They can also act in symbiosis with roots, making nutrient-gathering by plants more efficient.

Like lichens, fungi are often very specific about the trees that they will grow on, so orchards are likely to have a proliferation of apple, pear and stone-fruit fungal specialists.

In addition to wood-loving fungi, orchards are also a refuge for slow-developing grassland species. Sensitive to chemicals and preferring short grass, waxcap fungi are increasingly rare in the UK, but they are a good indicator of good-quality 'unimproved' grassland and undisturbed soil.

A cabaret of beasts

A diverse menagerie of pollinators, pests, predators and prey lives in the orchard ecosystem. They overlap and interact, both in where they live and in what they eat, so it makes sense to discuss them all together.

Living and breeding

Birds, bats and social insects such as bees roost and breed in orchard trees and hedges, and as older trees develop pits and cracks they become more and more attractive to these animals. Fissured and flaking bark is a refuge for spiders, lacewings and hibernating ladybirds, while some hoverflies lay their eggs in damp cavities.

Standing deadwood and fallen branches support insects that depend on decaying timber. The stag beetle, *Lucanus cervus*, is one of the UK's largest beetles. It spends up to 7 years in its vulnerable larval stage, eating its way through soft, decaying wood, before pupating and emerging as a handsome adult. Ground beetles are another group that thrives in leaf litter and crumbling wood. Although relatively common in Europe, one of Britain's rarest beetles is the bronzy-green noble chafer beetle,

Old wood, high moisture levels and a stable environment help all sorts of organisms to get a foothold.

HIDDEN TREASURES

Having been declared extinct in the UK, the golden-eye lichen, *Teloschistes chrysophthalmus*, was rediscovered in a Herefordshire orchard in 2007.

The soil-level orchard community benefits from a lack of digging and ploughing.

In continental Europe, hollow trees are a valuable nesting site for the threatened hoopoe.

Hazelnuts in the hedgerow are a tasty meal for small animals and humans alike.

On acid soil, the diverse mix of grasses and flowers includes clover, vetch and sweet vernal grass.

Gnorimus nobilis, which is almost entirely limited to old orchards.

Between the trees, a rich grassland habitat is able to develop in the undisturbed soil. This supports bees, solitary wasps and hornets, together with small mammals that nest in tussocks and burrows, and the moth and butterfly larvae that dine on meadow and hedgerow species.

Hunting and eating

The food web in the orchard is intricate. Blossom provides nectar for the bees and hoverflies, which pollinate the fruit in return. Butterflies sip at wild-flowers. Small birds peck at ripe fruit, and wind-falls sustain blackbirds and fieldfares for weeks or months after the human harvest is done.

In the canopy, leaves provide shelter for aphids and caterpillars – a feast for ladybirds, lacewings and insectivorous birds. Meanwhile the same bark crevices and soft wood that appeal so much to insects become a perfect foraging ground for woodpeckers, nuthatches and treecreepers.

At soil level, the damp understorey yields juicy slugs, snails and earthworms for ground beetles, shrews, hedgehogs, moles and thrushes. By night, bats swoop low after mosquitoes and night-flying pests like the codling moth. Bigger predators too are abroad: owls hunt unwary rodents, and they won't say no to a fat bat either, if they can catch one.

Plants

The orchard floor community can include meadow grasses such as Yorkshire fog (*Holcus lanatus*) or crested dogstail (*Cynosurus cristatus*), and grass

Even non-orchard-specialists like the rose chafer beetle can be tempted by the scrub and grassland of this rich and accommodating environment.

Rosehips and other berries are a good winter food supply for hungry birds and mice.

parasites like yellow rattle (*Rhinanthus minor*), together with flowers like vetch, oxeye daisies, clover, knapweed (*Centaurea nigra*) and butter-cups. Cowslips and primroses form buttery pools under hedges, and snowdrops are a welcome herald of spring.

Hedges provide for both wildlife and wildflowers. Tucked into the moss and leafmould there may be violets, greater stitchwort (*Stellaria holostea*) and pignut (*Conopodium majus*). Honeysuckle, old man's beard (*Clematis vitalba*), ivy and wild roses tangle upwards, creating dense roosting and hibernating spaces, nectar for insects and other food supplies in the form of brambles, sloes, wild plums, hips and haws.

Mistletoe

As a symbol of vitality and fertility, mistletoe (*Viscum album*) is deeply embedded in European folklore. While now mainly associated with Christmas, its historical roles included folk medicine, rites of crop protection and warding off witches.

Mistletoe thrives in a humid environment and is usually found on soft-barked trees like apple. A hemiparasite, it takes minerals and water from the host tree, while the green stems and leaves produce sugars by photosynthesis. It used to be very common in the fruit-growing regions of England, but, with the decline of traditional orchard management, mistletoe has also suffered. Each ball of mistletoe creates a micro-ecosystem: specific

Mistletoe is a parasite and should be regularly harvested to stop it damaging the trees. It produces male and female plants, and you will need one of each to get berries.

Planting young trees gives the wildlife something to move into in a few years' time.

species include the mistletoe marble moth (or mistletoe tortrix moth), *Celypha woodiana*.

Mistletoe is usually spread by birds such as the mistle thrush, which wipe the sticky berries from their beaks on to a branch, or excrete them after eating them. The ripe seeds adhere to the branch and germinate, penetrating the bark to fuse with the cambium. With ripe berries, a moist location and good light, it is quite possible to seed orchards and garden trees with mistletoe.

Encouraging wildlife in the orchard

There is plenty that can be done to make an area attractive to wild animals and plants. The key thing is to understand what they need and why.

Replenish the tree stock. Planting young trees on a regular basis builds up a profile of trees of different ages; this will provide a habitat continuum over a long period.

Leave dead and decaying wood. Old trees are disproportionately valuable in their environmental contribution. If you do need to take an old tree down, then create a stack of logs from it, to maintain the habitat.

Manage the grass. Grazing or cutting for hay will keep the grass reasonably short. A grass length of 5-10cm (2-4") gives plenty of depth for invertebrates to shelter, yet is short enough for fungi and seedlings to emerge.

Comma butterflies cluster to enjoy sweet fermenting fruit that has been deemed unsuitable for human consumption.

In the absence of grazers, scything the grass beneath the trees is quiet, environmentally friendly and gives escaping wildlife a fighting chance.

Lay off the chemicals. Herbicides, insecticides and fertilizers will all damage populations of wild-flowers, pollinators, insect predators and fungi. This occurs either by direct action of the chemical, by reduction of a host species, or because an increase in nutrients favours vigorous grasses and weeds, outcompeting desirable plants.

Leave fallen fruit. Don't be too rigorous when it comes to clearing up the windfalls. They are a useful source of food for birds and butterflies, and for the wasps and hornets that deal so effectively with pests early in the year. Generosity pays.

Preserve hedges and ditches. Boundaries are another wildlife habitat. Hedges supply additional roosting space and food for insects, birds and small mammals. A water source such as a ditch, pond or stream encourages amphibians. Even the cracks in walls can provide a home for small creatures.

Think about the big picture. Consider the ways in which each element interacts within and beyond the orchard, and what it needs. Are there wildlife corridors to connect habitats? Are there food sources all year round? There is no point in planting lots of lovely nectar-rich flowers to encourage adult pollinators, while continuing to hoik out nearby weeds that are the primary food source for the larval stage of those same insects.

A HOLISTIC SYSTEM

In the simple sketch on the preceding pages, we have looked at some of the organisms that live in an orchard and the ways in which they interact. But I find environmental reductionism uncomfortable. Breaking an ecosystem down into its component parts tells you what is there but does not necessarily confer an understanding of how it works.

In the natural world, nothing exists in isolation. Everything lives on or in or under something else. Remove one element and the entire system suffers. Why bother with grass and meadow flowers, if it is apples we want? Well, because the bees that pollinate the fruit need something to eat later in the year as well. Why keep the untidy old trees when they are no longer productive? Because they are home to beetles whose very existence has value, as well as providing overwintering spots for helpful creatures that clear out the pests.

When it comes to wildlife, orchards and gardening in general, I can't help feeling that there is more sense, as well as more poetry, in being

At this orchard restoration project at Grim's Dyke in Harrow Weald, logs from felled trees have been piled up to create habitat.

ABOVE LEFT:
A chilly ladybird catches some sun on a late winter's day.

ABOVE RIGHT:
A bee gorges itself on summer knapweed.

part of the system rather than external to it. In our luxuriously abundant world, why impose the rigour of producer and consumer when we, too, are part of the dialogue?

The green-shadowed, cider-drenched orchard might exist without us, but we are a dependent part of everything it represents ... the lackadaisical insect hum; the soft rustle-thud of earth-bound apples. As a species, we are prone to posturing role-play, yet without the supporting cast of hoverflies and robins, the vast biomass that underpins the higher animals, the choir of bumblebees and the slow pulse of seasons, there would not only be no fruit to pick but also no humankind to know.

And beyond the satisfaction of harvesting and pruning, there is much quieter joy to be had in the orchard: in simply spotting a hairy caterpillar; watching comma butterflies drunkenly congregating on rotten apples; applauding the defiant iridescence of winter moss. We are a small part of a harmonious whole, so we should take our place in the natural order of things. We do well to accept and enjoy our Eden.

GENETIC DIVERSITY IN CULTIVATED FRUIT

After bananas, apples are the world's second-most-popular cultivated fruit: a crop of huge social and economic importance. Over the years, many thousands of varieties have been named: Brogdale holds over

2,200 that are deemed to be important, and thousands more would have existed in local commerce. Meanwhile, an unsubstantiated and possibly inflated inventory recorded about 14,000 in nineteenth-century America, as discussed in Chapter 1. Other countries would have had varieties of their own.

Yet, in the whole world, the number of cultivated varieties now hovers around a relatively modest 7,500, of which the formerly mighty USA grows only about 100 commercially. The total number of apples produced is enormous, but the number of varieties has crashed.

Commercial growers usually favour attractive and evenly sized modern hybrids, and trees that crop early in their lives. Varieties are often dictated by large retailers, responding to demand stoked by multi-million-pound advertising campaigns. The criteria for commercially viable fruit are strict: they must store well and have thick skin to reduce the risk of damage in transit. A good deep colour that does not show bruising is a bonus. These demands have an impact not only on the perception of fruit among the broader population but also on the very nature and viability of the fruit tree species themselves.

A genetic whirlpool

For commercial growers, efficient production and a consistent and reliable apple is everything, and as apple-growing intensified in the twentieth century, certain varieties came to prominence. The importance of the export market, coupled with relatively recent changes in the ways in which people source both groceries and information, has had far-reaching effects on the number of varieties commonly available.

Red Delicious originated in America in 1880. Originally known as Hawkeye, it was acquired as a commercial variety by Stark Nurseries, who renamed it 'Stark Delicious', the 'Red' being added only when Golden Delicious joined the stable in 1914. This apple is brightly coloured and cosmetically perfect, and the trees are heavy and precocious croppers. Aggressively marketed, Red Delicious came to dominate sales in America and abroad, and by the 1980s it represented three-quarters of the apple harvest in Washington State.

The very diversity that enabled seedling fruit to be successful in the diaspora of the European, American and Australian continents is becoming compromised.

Public demand, driven by advertising, driven in turn by commercial efficiency, sets up a ripple effect. Perfectly good varieties fall by the wayside as growers follow a market largely beyond their control. Thus, the number of varieties available is progressively reduced – along with consumer awareness. This is a tragedy for gastronomy and knowledge, but, more importantly, the reduction in genetic variation also impacts on the potential of fruit stocks to produce offspring that can withstand environmental changes.

In *The Book of Apples*, Joan Morgan writes: "While the apple's symbolic, religious, decorative and patriotic appeal all contributed to [its success], it is ultimately the apple's remarkable adaptability that has given it dominion." And this is a key point. The very diversity that enabled seedling fruit to be successful in the diaspora of the European, American and Australian continents is becoming compromised.

BELOW LEFT: This Bramley's Seedling at RHS Garden Wisley was grown from graft-wood from the original tree. 95 per cent of the cooking apples sold in Britain are Bramleys.

BELOW RIGHT: Try beautiful local apples, even if you have never heard of them!

Commercially successful fruit such as Golden Delicious, Red Delicious, Granny Smith and Bramley are seedlings of unknown parentage, but their carefully selected progeny, like Braeburn, Gala, Jazz and Fuji, are ubiquitous. The benefits of perpetuating desirable characteristics comes at a price: continued inbreeding makes the genetic pool smaller and smaller; less and less adaptable to change.

Cultivated fruit trees can become sickly; close-quarters living and inbreeding leaving them vulnerable to bacterial and insect pestilence. Growers defend as best they can, but pests are smart. They evolve continuously, and if the trees don't have the resilience to respond effectively to new or more virulent threats, there are severe implications. To future-proof fruit stocks, out-breeding is essential.

THE TOLL OF CONSERVATIVE CHOICES

The modern requirement for produce to store well over long periods is, alongside physical perfection and good looks, a key influence on the choice of fruit in our shops. Fruit that will not store well or looks a bit funny is just not grown commercially, no matter how scrumptious it may be. This situation becomes self-perpetuating.

I have found that you can walk into a shop with a tray of beautiful local apples, and they ask if you have any Cox's Orange Pippins instead. Now, Cox's Orange Pippin is a great apple, but it may not be better than the ones in the tray. But whether Cox's are better looking, tastier, will keep longer or can be grown successfully in the local climate is not relevant in this conversation. What retailers want is an apple that they and their customers have heard of.

Personally, I am in favour of using an apple to promote itself. Cox's Orange Pippin won't thrive in my soggy orchard, so I grow its offspring Sunset as a more reliable alternative. It looks and tastes broadly similar to Cox's. And if you walk into a shop and say clearly "Would you like to stock these apples? They are called Sunset and are related to Cox's Orange Pippin", most people don't hear the words *called Sunset and are related to*, and are happy to stock them. It's a funny old world.

WILD FRUIT UNDER THREAT

In light of today's environmental challenges, and acknowledging the proportionally minute number of apple varieties in mainstream cultivation, there is new focus on the original fruit forests in Central Asia: an important gene bank. In the same way that botanists and breeders are looking to the Andes for wild potato and tomato varieties that may carry genes conferring resistance to blight, scientists are looking to the 'Eve' populations of tree fruit for such beneficial attributes.

But the wild apple is under threat. The mountains that once were wooded wilderness are now encroached upon by domestic herbivores and by agricultural and urban expansion. It is estimated that in the last 30 years, 70 per cent of the original population of wild apple trees has disappeared, catapulting *Malus sieversii* on to the International Union of

LESSONS FROM HISTORY

We know that populations with low genetic variation are more susceptible to environmental change and disease than are more diverse populations. One extreme example of such vulnerability led to the Irish Potato Famine of the 1840s, which is estimated to have killed a million people and caused over a million more to emigrate.

Because it is easy to propagate potatoes vegetatively, the commonly grown variety was all one clone – a clone that had low resistance to the fungal disease *Phytophthora infestans*, or potato blight. When conditions were right, the disease swept across Ireland, causing economic ruin and widespread starvation. Resistant varieties existed in the wild, but these were not selected and bred into the commercial gene pool until much later.

Apples do not breed true, so they tend to be propagated by grafting – essentially, the fruiting part of the tree is genetically identical to the original bearer of its name. If only a small number of highly selected individuals are allowed to flower and fruit, and only these are allowed to interbreed, the wild-type evolution and resistance in the cultivated population diminishes, with potentially catastrophic results.

Nature's Red List of threatened species. Those trees that remain are clustered in gorges, peaks and other refuges.

What's more, domestic fruit is now locally common, and wild–domestic hybrids arise: the modern fruit infiltrating and eroding the original gene pool. In order to safeguard the future of fruit-breeding and, potentially, to combat yet-to-emerge pests and diseases, the forest remnants need conserving.

The US National Collection of apples is located on the campus of Cornell University's New York State Agricultural Experiment Station. One of the largest and most genetically diverse collections in the world, it includes hundreds of specimens of *M. sieversii* collected from the wild apple forest of Central Asia. Under experimental conditions, it is becoming apparent that a percentage of these have genetic resistance to diseases such as fireblight, phytophthora and scab. Interbreeding these with existing commercial varieties could have huge benefits for the world's apple industry.

LOCAL AND HERITAGE VARIETIES

As commercial forces pare down the widely available fruit stocks on the one hand, while desperately trying to conserve the gene pool on the other, there are further repositories of genetic information all around us.

In the centuries that fruit has been cultivated, every region – or indeed, every village – is likely to have had its own apple variety (of which more in Chapter 4). Legions must have been lost, while a few have become well known – but what of the rest?

A proportionally large number of cultivars bear the collectible mantle of 'heritage fruit'. These may not be particularly commercially viable, but are well loved nonetheless. British varieties include Devonshire Quarrenden and Cornish Aromatic; Worcester Pearmain and the delicate Reverend W. Wilks. But others persist under the radar of conservationists –

The pretty, hardy Devonshire Quarrenden was first recorded in the 1690s.

perhaps just a few individuals which grow on in half a dozen local gardens and are preserved in the village as 'our tree'.

Thus, the world of fruit operates on several levels: from commercial varieties in the big-business spotlight to the much-esteemed older, heritage varieties in small orchards. Beyond this is a rich underworld of 'black-market', non-standard fruit that is recognized only locally. Finally, there are the seedling remnants of orchards consigned to history, persisting in the feral offspring of hedgerow wildings. Here is our mother lode: from this stock, individuals of superb flavour and unparalleled hardiness may emerge at any point.

Old fruit good, new fruit bad?

There are romantic associations with heritage varieties. But just because a fruit is old does not automatically make it good. It might once have been the best of its type,

Court Pendu Plat is a very old apple, dating from at least the 1600s if not before. The name comes from the French: 'court pendu' referring to its short pendant or pedicel, and 'plat' denoting its distinctive flattened shape.

but, even in ordinary plant-breeding timescales, the 'best' plants are frequently superseded by better ones.

This does not contradict the argument that the gene pool should be conserved – but nor is striving for better varieties inherently evil. Fruit like apples and pears don't breed true, so those that have stood the test of time are those worth perpetuating by grafting. And there is always room for a better fruit. Pollination experiments have been a feature of fruit development for a thousand years or more. Medieval monks did it; so did eighteenth-century horticulturists. Modern breeders selecting for desirable attributes to create new strains is just the latest phase.

The arguments could go on indefinitely: modern versus artisan; traditionalist versus pioneer. But this misses the point, which is that it is good to be able to grow fruit successfully, and we need to keep our

NATIONAL FRUIT COLLECTION, BROGDALE

The British National Fruit Collection at Brogdale holds over 4,000 varieties of fruit: 2,200 apple cultivars, together with pears, plums, cherries, medlars and nuts. These comprise both well-known varieties and footnotes to fruit history which might otherwise be extinct – fruit once popular but which slid from its zenith as fashions changed and better varieties emerged.

The fruit here may not be very good-looking. It may or may not taste terribly good compared to others. The fruits may be uneven and small, blemish easily, crop lightly or irregularly, suffer from damage from pests or diseases, or all of the above. These are, therefore, not particularly suitable for commercial production and may not find widespread favour.

Yet this is not just a museum. And its value is not just that it represents a conservatory of unusual fruit, in case of future need. It is also a fabulous, visitable, tastable resource and hub of knowledge – a fruity theme park with one foot in the past and the other in the future. (See Resources for details.)

options open. In some gardens, small, quick-to-crop newer varieties might be a pleasing choice. It is also good to celebrate local character and national heritage. And the day that children cease planting pips and cherishing the unknowable fruit of the future will be dark indeed.

IF NOT US THEN WHO?

Much of this chapter has been about big ideas. Global commercial fruit-growing; genetic conservation or erosion on a grand scale. The environmental benefits of orchards that have perhaps stood for hundreds of years. Evolutionary development and complex population interactions that have taken aeons to emerge in their current form.

How, then, can an individual have any impact on this? If not a land-owner or a custodian of a traditional orchard, how can the ordinary person hope to have any influence on the bigger picture? The answer is: surprisingly easily.

We have already seen, in the last chapter, how informal patchworks of urban planting can make up a much larger whole, and how, even in a small garden or at a local or community level, our actions can help support the environment. It is the little things that make a difference. It might be wonderful to have a whole orchard, but just a few trees to feed the wildlife, or to conserve local or rare varieties, is a valuable contribution.

A small tree in an ordinary border in an ordinary garden feeds the bees when in blossom and the gardener when in fruit.

Whoever you are and wherever you live, here are some ways in which you can make a difference:

❋ **Retain that old apple tree in the garden and plant a new one.** This way you both conserve the existing habitat and extend it. Blossom encourages pollinators, and insects will attract birds. Look over the fence and join the habitat dots with the neighbours: together you may already be building a decent orchard mosaic without realizing it.

❋ **Preserve your local varieties.** Plant them in a community orchard or, if space is an issue, get them grafted on to dwarfing rootstocks. Then the local genes will persist and their role in the community – both human and ecological – will be consolidated.

❋ **Support growers who produce local or heritage varieties.** Seek them out, pay them a visit, or buy fruit, juice or fruit products from their outlets. Consumer choices make a difference. Source local fruit from farmers' markets (and supermarkets where they offer it). Enjoy the unusual rather than simply demanding the well-known and ubiquitous.

* **Support local orchard conservation efforts.** Get involved in whatever way you are able. They may need help with planting trees, handing out leaflets, surveying the wildlife; they may want someone to get stuck into the pruning; or they may just appreciate people turning up on Apple Day.

* **Plug into local gleaning groups** if you produce more fruit than you can use. There may be cooperatives or individuals who will be glad to save waste, distribute food or make preserves.

Conservation is a global issue, but it is also a local one. The critical bit is helping the trees and their attendant wildlife in all its interesting diversity – giving them another base from which to operate and another opportunity to survive. The important thing is not *how* you plug into the green network. It is that you do it at all.

ABOVE LEFT:
School and community orchards can open up orchard gardening opportunities, including to those with little or no growing space of their own.

ABOVE RIGHT:
Attractive permanent labelling is a real advantage!

"Who knows but this chance wild fruit, planted by a cow or a bird on some remote and rocky hill-side, where it is as yet unobserved by man, may be the choicest of all its kind?"
HENRY DAVID THOREAU, *WILD APPLES* (1862)

In this restored walled garden the trees are a beautiful and still-productive feature.

Orchard consultant, designer, author and horticulture historian Tom Burford is on a mission to recapture the lost rich American apple culture. Having watched the industry moulder and decay during the middle of the twentieth century, he is now, an octogenarian, one of the pioneers for its resurrection: fusing the historic apple with today's emerging dynamic fruit industry.

His family has grown fruit in Virginia since 1715. Remembering this glorious past and its contribution to humankind, he closed his own nursery and orchard in 1997 and sallied forth to educate the masses on the subtleties of flavour and the nuances of variety, spear-heading a nationwide fruit revival.

"Sometimes I think I have cider flowing through my veins!" he says.

Paving the way for the planting of millions of trees of diverse varieties, by local orchard keepers serving local markets, Tom began teaching fruit-tree grafting to anyone who was interested. Thousands came to learn from 'Professor Apple'; thousands of new orchards dotted the landscape, and hundreds of new backyard fruit-tree nurseries blossomed.

"The big and beautiful bully of an apple that stymied diversity was the Red Delicious. In the nineteenth century it was a decent fruit, but now it is the cause of the largest compost heap in the world," he exclaims. *"Each week you buy a bag, take a bite of one and think 'oh, this is not very good', so it goes in the trash. The rest rot and are dumped in the compost and the next week you do the same thing. In a year you have at least 52 bags of rotted Red Delicious apples – promotion and marketing prevailing over flavour and enjoyment."*

An active supporter of Slow Food America and local farmers' markets, Tom is author of *Apples of North America* (2013) and co-author of the Brooklyn Botanic Garden book *The Best Apples to Buy and Grow* (2005). He continues to spread the word through lectures and workshops, while exploring the landscape for 'lost' fruit varieties of merit to return to commerce.

"The apple is now taking its rightful place as one of the great food commodities of the world," he says. *"Flavoursome varieties are becoming available once more, and the apple adventure offers untold colours, shapes, sizes and tastes. But for me, after biting into hundreds of them, my favourite is always the last one I ate!"*

CHAPTER FOUR

ORCHARDS IN THE COMMUNITY

This chapter looks at orchards and fruit that may be more widely accessible than domestic or commercial collections. It considers ownership and enjoyment of fruit resources, the traditions of the past and the opportunities of the future. It is about growing, sharing and foraging – but, more than that, it is also about environment, the local economy and the fruit heritage that exists in each neighbourhood.

Tap into the networks of local food enthusiasts, and there is no such thing as a fruit glut. Neighbours who cook; farmers' markets and increasingly enlightened local retailers; schools inspired by Apple Day – people are surprisingly willing to share; to both give and receive. Communities, delighted by the opportunities that local produce presents, are reinventing themselves for modern times.

This chapter is also about people collectively taking ownership of their 'place' – which is achievable regardless of the nature of the community. It is about the power of the group and about harnessing the will and energy to conserve or generate a sense of local distinctiveness. It is also about reconnecting with the landscape on a personal level.

A favourite tree provides a tasty snack on the way into town.

A SHARED RESOURCE

The concept of 'orchard in the community' covers a wide range of situations. Some community orchards are crisply defined, while other types, such as orchard restorations and relict fragments, are less precisely labelled. We will discuss formal 'community orchards' and local food production later in this chapter, together with the folklore and customs that create distinctiveness. But first it is useful, for the purposes of this book, to loosely define orchard types – as follows (from most to least organized):

✳ **Dedicated community orchards.** These are planted in a field or urban location specifically acquired for the purpose. They tend to be relatively new and often well organized.

Autumn heralds generous offerings on garden walls.

❊ **Integrated community orchards.** These are established within the framework of an existing community space: perhaps in a community garden, allotment or school garden. Many villages have preserved old orchards by adopting them and taking 'ownership'. This sort of community orchard might be more varied than the previous sort, with older and newer trees planted at different times.

❊ **Incidental orchards.** This describes the haphazard landscape trees; the remnants of orchards that have been built upon and the trees that are left when buildings are no more. It includes hedges that provide edible fruit, and abstract wayside clusters. While not officially defined as a community orchard, these are de facto orchards in the community.

❊ **The landscape as an extended community orchard.** This notion applies to all those trees that produce fruit that can be grazed upon or nibbled: the mulberry in the park; the sweet chestnuts that drop into lay-bys; the fig leaning over that high wall. It includes sloes and wilding apples in the hedge, and cherries planted as street trees.

The most organized orchards in the community are those where residents plant up a dedicated space for a definite purpose, like this Urban Orchard Project planting day.

The form an orchard in the community takes and how it is used depends greatly on the type of community, the individuals within it and the trees themselves. But, irrespective of the type of orchard and the formality of the arrangement, fruit in the community is a shared resource, and this means that both its benefits and its care and protection must be shared. This is the case whether one is picking sloes off a hedgerow, caring for a village orchard, or using unorthodox collections of foraged or garden fruit in a community jam-making enterprise.

FORAGING

Foraging is the practice of searching for food rather than procuring it in some other way. It is the 'gathering' part of being a hunter-gatherer. In the modern sense, it is the gathering of edibles for personal use and not for profit. The ethos of foraging is founded upon the concept of our landscape as an extended community orchard.

Some landowners and organizations don't object to foraging on a small scale. The National Trust runs occasional foraging courses, and the Woodland Trust permits foraging for personal use in its woods (but not in Sites of Special Scientific Interest).

"I find I've drifted this way myself, evolving into a wayside nibbler. I like lucky finds, small wayside gourmet treats. I relish the shock of the new taste, that first bite of an unfamiliar fruit . . . Often the catch is apples, wayside wildings sprung from thrown-away cores and bird droppings. They seem to catch everything that's exhilarating about foraging: a sharpness of taste, and of spirit; an echo of the vast, and mostly lost, genetic diversity of cultivated fruits; a sense of place and season. I've found apples that tasted of pears, fizzed like sherbet, smelt of quince . . . But it's the finding of them, the intimacy with the trees and the places that they grow, a heightened consciousness of what they need to survive, that are just as important."

RICHARD MABEY, *FOOD FOR FREE* (2012)

It is sometimes argued that foraging is just pillaging the countryside; that it is environmental theft for personal gain and will inevitably lead to loss of biodiversity and habitat degradation. However, foragers are often exactly the people who have a good understanding of, and connection to, the landscape. Unregulated collection of species for commercial gain – now that *is* a problem. As is taking a large portion of a population or damaging the parent plant and the surrounding environment. Greed, stupidity and ignorance will ruin the party, but taking a small tithe of an abundance will not.

So, be gentle and take your place – not as a dominant predator but as part of the greater community of plants, wildlife and people, to ensure that there will be abundance again tomorrow. (See tips on page 111.)

Foraging and the law

All land belongs to someone. Whether it is The National Trust, the local authority, a private landowner or any other entity. So, is foraging theft? In the UK, the Theft Act 1968 states that "A person who picks mushrooms growing wild on any land, or who picks flowers, fruit or foliage from a plant growing wild on any land, does not (although not in possession of the land) steal what he picks, unless he does it for reward or

SCRUMPING

In the UK, scrumping is part of the cultural heritage. Depicted in literature as a practice engaged in by rosy-cheeked scamps, the term describes the minor theft of fruit, often apples, and implies a light-hearted rather than felonious activity.

According to *The Concise Oxford English Dictionary*, the word is from the nineteenth-century dialect word 'scrump', meaning a withered apple. Scrumpy, meanwhile, is a strong cider made from small fruit.

The apple blossom cascading over the towpath of the Kennet and Avon Canal promises a forager's harvest later in the year.

FORAGING TIPS

A little casual grazing along the hedgerows is unlikely to cause trouble, but if you want to harvest more than a snack or a pocketful – say, you want larger quantities for jam – seek permission from the landowner or whoever is in charge. If the land is owned by an organization, there may be instructions on its website. Ensure that you keep to the spirit of true foraging by observing these basic guidelines:

✳ Don't strip the tree. Wild fruit is an important food source for a wide range of wildlife, and it is community-spirited to leave some for the next person who travels that way.

✳ Tread lightly and be respectful: greed and vandalism are not cool.

✳ Be open and generous: if your whole landscape is an orchard, then it is only right to share it and inspire other people to value it.

Use common sense:

✳ Choose fruit that is high up and clean, away from the splashback of cars or passing dog-walks. Avoid trees growing on industrial or obviously contaminated land.

✳ Don't try to reach fruit that is growing in dangerous places.

✳ If foraging on the roadside, consider investing in a hi-viz jacket!

✳ Stick with what you can clearly identify. Most tree fruit is easy to spot, but if you are in any doubt, or in an unfamiliar country, check with an expert.

Pick up a good book on foraging. Richard Mabey's *Food for Free* is a classic, or try *The Thrifty Forager: Living off your local landscape* by Alys Fowler or *Wild Food: A complete guide for foragers* by Roger Phillips.

The power of the people can be harnessed to optimize local foraging. For example, Oxford Wild Food has a crowd-sourced map of good locations and what to find there; declaring on Twitter that "Oxford isn't a city with added fruit trees, it's an orchard with added houses." At the other end of the scale, FallingFruit.org is a huge collaborative map of the global urban harvest, of various sorts. Other organizations are listed in the online resources page for this book (see page 212 for web link).

Gleaning an orchard ensures that nothing goes to waste.

GLEANING AND FOOD REDISTRIBUTION

Gleaning is the salvaging of the portion of harvest that might otherwise be left in the field. It was common in the past among orphans, widows and the poor, and, with increasing awareness of the waste that results from 'imperfect' crops being rejected, it is seeing a resurgence.

The Gleaning Network UK, and the parallel European organization, the Gleaning Network EU, brings together volunteers to help salvage 'unwanted' fruit and vegetables. Between 2012 and 2015, 2 million portions of food in the UK were saved and redirected to people in need. There are similar projects in the USA. This approach is increasingly seen as a viable way of keeping food banks topped up and helping to support the vulnerable.

A network of organizations such as FareShare in the UK also collect unsold food from retailers and redistribute it to charities, contributing to 16.6 million meals a year.

> The history of orchards is the history of mankind. In the past, they would have played an important role in the community, providing regular seasonal employment, a harvest to celebrate, and food to preserve and store.

for sale or other commercial purpose." But local bye-laws and conservation legislation make for a complicated legal position.

In the USA, while foraging is established in cities and rural areas, the legal position varies. In some towns it is discouraged or prohibited as a 'rural' activity, and it is illegal in some State Parks. For more information, seek out local foraging groups and check local or regional legislation. Park websites may have information on gleaning and foraging policies.

The way forward is a combination of common sense and being open and polite. A sense of respect is key: for the plants whose fruits are being harvested, for the animals that depend on them, and for the landowner.

ORCHARD LORE

The history of orchards is the history of mankind. In the past, they would have played an important role in the community, providing regular seasonal employment, a harvest to celebrate, and food to preserve and store. This was a resource to use to its fullest extent. Beyond the mundane husbandry, there were spirits to placate, ills to medicate and rites of fruitfulness to perform.

Wassailing

In Anglo-Saxon English, 'waes hail' means 'be you healthy'. Wassailing has been used for hundreds if not thousands of years, to wake the trees and ensure a good harvest. It usually takes place between New Year and the old Twelfth Night, which, before the introduction of the Gregorian

SING AND BE MERRY

There are various wassail songs from around Britain. Some, like The Wassail Song, have become linked with Christmas. Others are secular or even pre-Christian in origin.

The Wassail Song

Here we come a-wassailing
Among the leaves so green,
Here we come a-wandering
So fair to be seen.

Chorus
Love and joy come to you,
And to you your wassail too,
And God bless you and send you
a happy New Year.
And God send you a happy New Year.

The Apple Tree Wassail
(from Somerset)

Old apple tree, we'll wassail thee,
And hoping thou wilt bear.
The Lord does know where we shall be
To be merry another year.
To blow well and to bear well,
And so merry let us be;
Let ev'ry man drink up his cup
And health to the apple tree.

calendar in 1752, fell on what is now 17th January. The tradition is still practised today.

The oldest or best tree is chosen as the orchard guardian and its roots are ceremonially nourished with cider. Pieces of toast are then placed in the branches by the Wassail Queen or the youngest boy, the Tom Tit, to honour and feed the robin, which represents the good spirits.

The revellers fire shotguns through the branches or bang vigorously on saucepans to frighten the evil spirits away. They serenade the trees with traditional wassail songs and partake liberally from a communal wassail bowl containing hot cider, sweetened and spiced, topped with slices of toast as sops. An alternative wassail ritual concerns the villagers going door to door, singing and drinking the health of those they visit, and generally kicking up a rumpus.

The roots of wassailing may go back a very long way. A Celtic myth sees apple trees as providers of life and energy, linked to rebirth after winter. Such rites as taking an earthenware cup of wassail and roasted crab apples, drinking half then throwing cup and contents at the tree, are sometimes represented as a sacrifice to Pomona, the Roman goddess of fruit.

Magic and mythology

The gods are pretty consistent on the subject of apples: they are magical and significant fruit, and many deities have associations with apples – or with a fruit that has generically become accepted as an apple.

In Norse legend, the goddess Idunna was the keeper of the apples of the gods, which they ate to remain young if they felt age approaching.

In Greek mythology, Paris made a major diplomatic error when Eris, the goddess of trouble, threw an apple inscribed 'for the fairest one' into a wedding party. It was claimed by Hera, Athena and Aphrodite, and to sort out the ensuing celestial cat fight, Zeus asked Paris to judge who was the most beautiful. Since only foolish mortals play fair, the three goddesses tried to bribe him. Aphrodite got her way – and the apple – when she offered him Helen of Sparta, the most beautiful woman in the world. Menelaus's attempts to get her back sparked the Trojan War.

ABOVE: Apples have not always favoured the righteous. They spelled trouble for Snow White and for Adam and Eve.

BELOW: Cold weather at the time the sloes are flowering is known as a 'blackthorn winter'.

Health associations

Apples and other fruit have long been used in cottage remedies. Over time, the lines between magic and medicine, between effective treatment and comfortingly embedded ritual, have become blurred.

In folk medicine, rheumatism could be cured by application of a rotten apple, while warts could be treated by rubbing with two halves of an apple that were then buried. Herbalists

In France, the medlar tree protected houses from enchantment and put witches to flight. Medlars appear in the literature of Chaucer and Shakespeare.

use apple bark as an astringent tonic for heartburn and bleeding gums, while in 1653 Culpeper advised in his *Complete Herbal* that "An infusion of sliced apples with their skins in boiling water, a crust of bread, some barley, and a little mace or all-spice, is a very proper cooling diet drink in fevers."

In the *Herball* of 1633, Gerard noted: "There is an ointment made with the pulp of apples and swine's grease and rosewater, which is used to beautify the face, and take away the roughness of the skin, called in shops pomatum of the apples whereof it is made." Today, cider vinegar is often touted as a cure-all, apparently dispelling dandruff and whitening teeth (presumably by slowly dissolving them), controlling blood sugar and reducing wrinkles. If overcome with healthy scepticism, it might be best to stick to using it for killing weeds and cleaning armour.

Sloes are another country remedy. Gerard's *Herball* advises that "The juice of Sloes do stop the belly, the lashe and bloody fluxe, the inordinate course of womens termes, and all other issues of blood in man or woman." Yet wild cherries are frankly alarming: he goes on to warn that "they conteine bad juice, they very soone putrifie, and do ingender ill bloud, by reason whereof they do not onely breede woormes in the belly, but troublesome agues, and often pestilent fevers". That said, in the first century AD, Dioscorides recommended cherry gum for coughs, a good complexion, good appetite and keen sight in his *De Materia Medica*.

But, as the maxim "An apple a day keeps the doctor away" implies, apples are good for us. They contain vitamin C to boost the immune system, and phenols, which reduce cholesterol. They are rich in soluble and insoluble

MODERN COTTAGE MEDICINE

Apples have been used as remedies within recent memory. As a small boy in the late 1940s, my father would be taken to see his Somerset relatives on the rattling bus along bumpy, winding country lanes. Unsurprisingly, he often went a bit green. "The apple in the top orchard is as hard as a brick and it is sharp, and it stays sharp no matter how long you keep it. They used to give me one of these to suck, and the sour juice seemed to stop me being travel-sick."

fibre. It has also been suggested by Cornell University researchers that quercetin, found in apples and other fruit, has a protective effect against neuro-degenerative disorders such as Alzheimer's disease.

These striking red catkins belong to a purple-leaved hazel tree in the nut orchard or nut 'plat' at RHS Garden Wisley.

REGIONALITY AND LOCAL FOCUS

From region to region, our landscape is coloured by its fruit heritage: the craft cider of the West Country and Normandy; the plums in Worcestershire; the French regions of Alsace and Lorraine and in Hungary. It is reflected in place names: in Germany we have the communities of Apfelbach, Apfelstetten, Eppelheim and Nussdorf (the last literally 'Nut village'), while in the USA there is an Apricot in Illinois and a Plumborough in Pennsylvania.

The English name Appleby derives from a combination of the Old Norse *apall*, meaning apple, and *byr*, a farm or settlement – so: Apple Farm or Orchard Farm. Settlements known as 'Apelbi' are recorded in both Lincolnshire and Leicestershire in the Doomsday Book. And, curiously, these old fruit-roots seem to have leapt oceans. There is a town

ABOVE LEFT: Some orchards strive to conserve old or local varieties. At Château du Rivau, the orchard has been planted with French varieties *à l'ancienne,* such as Pomme d'Api Noir and local Pépin de Bourgueil.

ABOVE RIGHT: High stone walls and steep, narrow flights of steps are characteristic of Bristol's streetscape.

called Appleby in South Dakota, another in Texas and a third in New Zealand. On 28th May 1635, a chap called William Appleby, aged 32 years, embarked in London on the ship *Speedwell,* bound for Virginia. Perhaps he did well.

The naming process works the other way around too. The Cornish Gilliflower and Devonshire Quarrenden hail their homeland, as do the apples Arkansas Black, Rhode Island Greening and Belle de Boskoop. A fruit's name may also be imbued with cultural significance: the Polish apple Kosztela has declined, but the smell and taste remain instantly recognizable to an older generation. In South Wales, Morgan Sweet, a Somerset eating and cider apple, has become enmeshed in Welsh folklore: the coal miners had very poor teeth, but as this apple is very soft it was a pleasant and manageable form of fresh fruit.

Local distinctiveness

What makes a place distinctive is elusive. It is tied into its climate and geography; its architecture and its socio-economic status; the social history, the wildlife, the landscape and vegetation. It is the 'feel' of a place, the patina of existence that accumulates with time. We saw in the last chapter how, in times gone by, every region had its own varieties of fruit. The erosion of such variety represents not only a loss of genetic diversity but also a loss of much cultural wealth.

The *Community Orchards Handbook* includes a lyrical description – quoted below – of the value of orchards to a locality and the results of their loss. Bitterly poignant, this is something that affects us all. It is why it is important to save old orchards in the community and plant new ones. Why we must find new ways to make them a valid and profitable part of society. By acquiring and passing on knowledge, we are maintaining a mindful chain of care.

Food security and the local economy

If a place does not produce its own food, the population is reliant upon a whole range of things that are beyond its control, including what is grown, how the crop is treated, how far it is transported and how much it costs. The consumers are effectively hostage to the demands of producers and distributors elsewhere.

And if those producers stop producing, or the transport network breaks down, a local community that is not geared up to feed itself rapidly runs

Planting trees and working together towards a common goal reconnects people with their landscape and builds social cohesiveness.

"As the touchstones in the everyday disappear, so do the stories prompted by their presence; the songs and customs annually enacted have neither theatre nor reason for repetition. We may not notice that the Red Rollo apple, Johnnie Moor plum or Late Treacle perry pear have been lost to the locality. But with their loss go the recipes that depended on the special properties of these fruits, along with the confidence of long knowledge of the right moment to pick, the length of time to store and the chemistry of mixing and cooking … Generations of hard-won wisdom about aspect and slope, soil and season, nuances of weather and variety dies with people who have nowhere to practise, no-one to tell."
SUE CLIFFORD AND ANGELA KING, *COMMUNITY ORCHARDS HANDBOOK* (2011)

into trouble. It was this concern for food security that led to the British Government campaign 'Dig for Victory' during the Second World War.

But if it is possible to grow at least some food locally, to make it affordable and easily available, then there is no argument not to do so. There are several key advantages:

✳ **Sustainable production.** Food miles are reduced and the local and global environment enhanced. This can improve biodiversity and reduce impacts on soil, air and water.

✳ **Increased connection.** The consumer knows where the food comes from and how it is grown.

✳ **Boost to the local economy.** Reducing waste and negotiating fair prices can benefit producers, while greater efficiency and shorter supply chains mean consumer savings. Local products are an asset to tourism.

✳ **Resilient communities.** The local food supply is more resilient when growers are part of a dynamic network, communicating with retailers and adapting quickly to demand. Collaboration and trading skills create opportunities, improving individual and social well-being and stimulating employment.

BELOW LEFT:
Local produce such as apple juice for sale adds character to festivals and other local events.

BELOW RIGHT:
Selling local food at festivals and farmers' markets provides a 'taste of the region' and can boost tourism and the local economy.

THE COOPERATIVE APPROACH

Tamar Grow Local in Devon and Cornwall is nurturing a cooperative approach to local food to help enterprises attain financial stability. One of the projects they work with is The Harrowbarrow and Metherell Community Orchard, on a former eucalyptus plantation.

Here, the removal of the trees has secured wood for a local wood-fuel cooperative and has enabled a livestock cooperative to keep their pigs there. Volunteers have worked to clear the land (with the help of the pigs), and have since begun to plant apple trees. With the addition of beehives to the orchard, the project represents a complementary system of land uses and enterprises, where all the projects work cooperatively but are not completely dependent on each other.

COMMUNITY ORCHARDS

Community orchards are enjoying a surge of popularity as a way of saving vulnerable old orchards and establishing new ones. Recognized as a valuable asset, they are used in many ways.

Every healthy community has places to meet and have events or discuss local issues, or which simply represent a common interest or goal. A community orchard provides just such a hub. It can host educational activities, and it can improve people's diets and give an insight into food production. It might be a hive of activity or a relaxing retreat – a place of work, play and celebration for people of all ages and backgrounds.

Community orchards succeed in housing estates, industrial estates, hospitals and schools, as well as in villages and other more traditional locations. Their primary use as an amenity, not purely as a source of fruit, allows them to be creatively managed. Their care is a shared responsibility, and the benefit or profit from the fruit is also shared.

ABOVE: If you need to protect the trees from farm animals, give yourself time to erect cages, or the triumph may be short-lived.

TOP: It is not just people who enjoy the orchard fruit!

Since community orchards were first mooted by Common Ground in 1992, they have sprung up in every collective space imaginable. And no two are the same: each community orchard is planted and cared for, accessed and harvested, in the way that works best for the people it serves.

How to make your community orchard happen

The *Community Orchards Handbook* (see Resources) gives detailed information on setting up a project and contains useful case studies. The following outline is a starting point.

Make a plan. Draft out what you are hoping to achieve. You can refer to this later to keep your project in focus. Consider location, helpers, funding, timeline and ultimate goals. What types of tree do you want? Be realistic about time, energy, money and the likely enthusiasm of your collaborators.

Where will the orchard be? Is it a new site or an orchard restoration? Who are the landowners and other stakeholders? Take into consideration access and aesthetics; can you reuse a piece of ground that has become derelict or an eyesore? Remember to think about what the trees will need to thrive.

What will the orchard be used for? Think objectives: what will you plant; how will it be grown and harvested? What will happen to the fruit? Will you include amenities like seating, a shelter, a fire pit or pond?

Get local support. Approach key members of the community with the idea. Explain the social, environmental and aesthetic benefits. Focus on the positives and be ready with solutions to potential objections.

Form a group and think about management. What are the arrangements for practical care? Who will be in charge of access and finances, risk assessments and insurance? How will decisions be made? How will you ensure a continuity of interest and expertise?

Think about fundraising. Trees, fences, signage and even photocopying cost money. Where will it come from? Will you ask for donations or hold fundraising events? Perhaps local businesses would sponsor a tree?

Start publicity and local engagement. Get people involved and enthusiastic via press, radio and word of mouth. Visit schools and contact the community council; hold an event to display plans and answer questions. Be specific. If you want funds, people with particular skills, volunteers for a work party or donations of trees or materials, ask for them.

Plant the trees. Organize your work party and order the trees. Don't forget to have enough spades, stakes, tree ties, rabbit guards and other essentials.

Celebrate! Have a launch party. Invite the community to enjoy the orchard. Wassail the new trees, light a fire, sing songs and mull some apple juice. The journey is just beginning.

School orchard projects

Schools across the UK are increasingly setting up orchards, and these enrich learning in all sorts of ways. There is plenty of help available – try the following.

✳ Fruit-full Schools in Scotland offers resources and planting information.

COMMUNITY ORCHARD TIPS AND IDEAS

Once you have your orchard, it can be used in all sorts of ways:

✳ Chickens roaming in the orchard produce free-range eggs – another source of local, traceable, affordable food.

✳ Installing beehives can help with pollinating the trees, and the honey can be sold locally.

✳ Include fruit for children: small pretty apples such as Pixie and pears such as Beth, which can be eaten off the tree.

✳ Make a local fruit map. Get a large plan of the area (village or neighbourhood) and identify trees and orchards, with a key for varieties and extra information. Putting it online and open access will allow people to interact.

✳ Encourage wildlife with log piles and standing deadwood.

✳ Issue a quarterly newsletter with news, events and updates to keep your supporters in the loop.

✳ Set up a website or blog. This will help publicize events, inform the community and chart the orchard's progress.

✳ Use the orchard as exhibition space: local sculptors or artists may want to be involved, or you could work with the community to make an artwork that 'belongs'.

※ The Urban Orchard Project has lots of tips and ideas on its website.

※ Learning through Landscapes has a booklet that distils the practical and inexpensive lessons learned from setting up dozens of school orchards.

※ The Mid-Kent Downs Orchard Project has some good community orchard resources for school use.

There are similar projects in countries around the world, which are interesting to look at for comparison. (They may also open up opportunities for international school orchard buddies.) Check out The Kohala Center in Hawaii, for example.

The gardening club at St Bartholomew's School in Newbury has an extensive orchard and garden.

APPLE DAY

Since Common Ground initiated Apple Day in 1990, this event has become widely celebrated, with thousands of events across the UK on or around 21st October. It is rooted in the idea of apples symbolizing heritage, ecology, diversity and distinctiveness, but it is also a jolly good opportunity to bring the community together in celebration, and is supported by organizations as diverse as The Wildlife Trusts and The National Trust, open gardens, schools, colleges and local authorities.

Events can be modest or huge, and can include games that have traditionally been associated with Hallowe'en, like apple-bobbing for children, together with longest-peel competitions, apple jugglers, taste tests and demonstrations, and the sale of jams, preserves and toffee apples. Participants include fruit-growers, juice- and cider-makers, experts in fruit identification, specialist fruit nurseries, and creators of apple-themed art.

There is some interesting background information about Apple Day on the Common Ground website, and an online search will quickly tell you what is happening in your local area.

Identifying fruit

Often at Apple Days there will be fruit specialists present to identify visitors' unknown apples. But, since fruit is variable, you can increase your chances of success by following a few simple rules:

✳ Take typical specimens and fruit that are mature. It is hard to identify a winter apple if it is presented in late summer.

✳ If the apples colour in the sunshine or when ripe, bring one of those along too.

✳ Choose apples that are in reasonably good condition and are of average size.

✳ Bring fruit complete with its stalk, and ideally with shoot and leaves.

✳ It will help if you can estimate the age of the tree or know when it was planted, as this will indicate whether it is a modern or older variety.

The RHS offers an apple-identifying service on a limited range of days – go to the RHS website and search on Fruit Identification. They also do pears, plums and other fruit, as does Brogdale Collections, for a fee.

ABOVE LEFT: Make your Apple Day go with a swing with toffee apples, spiced cider and face-painting.

ABOVE RIGHT: Apple-bobbing is a popular Apple Day activity, as visitors to West Green House in Hampshire discovered.

COMMUNITY JUICING

Egremont Russet waiting to be pressed.

The fruit is macerated and then poured into the pressing cloths that make up the 'cheese'.

Community juicing schemes turn surplus fruit into cider and apple juice, pooling resources and salvaging fruit that might otherwise go to waste, for everyone to enjoy. It also creates a product that can potentially be sold to raise funds for charity or other projects.

There are several different ways it can work, for example:

✳ A local organization hires out an apple press to groups.

✳ You take your apples to someone with an apple press, and they collect together apples from various sources and press them for a fee. (You can often buy juice from them even if you have no apples.)

✳ Some community projects will accept your apples, give a proportion back in juice form – usually half – and sell the rest of the juice to cover their costs.

✳ A number of stakeholders buy pressing equipment jointly to use on a rota basis.

✳ Apple-juice demonstrations and services are common at Apple Days, and they may press your fruit while you wait.

PUBLIC GARDENS IN SLOTTSTRÄDGÅRDEN, SWEDEN

In the city of Malmö in southern Sweden, Slottsträdgården (Castle Park Gardens) has incorporated old Scanian varieties of fruit tree such as Hampus, Eldrött Duväpple, Maglemer and Filippa into the public gardens. "They were grafted on to a strong-growing Swedish A2 rootstock in 1996 to create large tall trees, which would result in a large visible flowering and numerous fruit," explains head gardener John Taylor. "I thought that large trees would be less susceptible to vandalism and social wear and tear, and this has worked out well."

The trees are underplanted with thousands of bulbs, and the area is used for picnicking and relaxing in summer and is the site of events such as Malmö Garden Show. "We would like to pick the fruit more, but the garden is open 24/7, which means many apples are picked by people at the weekend or in the evening," says John, who is relaxed about the public enjoying the fruit. "As gardeners we just accept this and have learned to live with it. It's not the end of the world!"

ORCHARD SQUARES COMMUNITY FOOD GARDEN, LONDON

In Lewisham, South London, the streets and buildings of the Orchard Estate are named after fruit. Yet Pitmaston House and Quince Road are in an ultra-deprived urban area, rather than a green and pleasant land. But since 2012 the residents have been working with The Urban Orchard Project, planting up orchards in underused green spaces with apples and plums, a gage, an apricot, pears and a mulberry.

The community is already seeing benefits: the gardening work improves physical and mental well-being and it has enabled people to get to know their neighbours, in some cases for the first time in 10 years of living on the estate. Several members of the group have become involved with training, and Orchard Leader Conrad Ellam is now a Master Orchardist, helping other orchards with pruning skills and wildlife features.

Regular events, such as Open Squares Weekend, work days, social get-togethers and barbecues, mean that the orchard group has created a place that now feels loved and cared for, and is a more enjoyable place in which to live and play.

Crocuses carpet the ground around the virescent walnut tree.

In the rolling Devon countryside, orchards of almonds and Asian pears are somewhat unusual, but Otter Farm is the product of an unusual vision. This is the home and experimental site of award-winning writer and climate-change gardener Mark Diacono.

His mission is to grow the best and tastiest food he can think of – both familiar fruit and nuts and an inspiring panoply of unusual and innovative varieties: from pecans to peaches; vegetables, vines and herbs.

"If you can eat it and it'll survive in the UK, it's likely to be here at Otter Farm," says Mark. *"Life is too short to grow unremarkable food, especially when there are so many delicious and beautiful possibilities."*

His idea is risky – gambling that the warming climate will make marginal crops viable. But it is also beautifully sustainable – growing delicious food organically without the chemical inputs and carbon load involved with transporting luxury food across the world.

"If we are innovative and bright-minded, we can do much to arrest and mitigate and take advantage of the climate change we are already committed to, and in such a way as to create productive landscapes and agricultural and horticultural employment," Mark explains.

"My aim is to show what's possible, to widen the British homegrown larder a little, and to encourage people to become more inquisitive about where their food comes from, as well as to support local producers who grow in the right way."

Spreading the word about the horticultural and gastronomic possibilities of such pioneering foods is at the core of Mark's work. In 2012, he opened online nursery Otter Farm Shop, to make new varieties and trained fruit forms available more widely, while his new project, Otter Farm Kitchen Garden School, will enable people to visit his exotic orchards and learn more about growing and using the fruit.

"The Otter Farm Kitchen Garden School allows us to throw the doors open on what we do, to inspire and enable as many people as possible to grow even a small amount of what they eat. There's pleasure enough in that in itself, but, equally importantly, it helps us take that crucial step to a more secure, healthier food system."

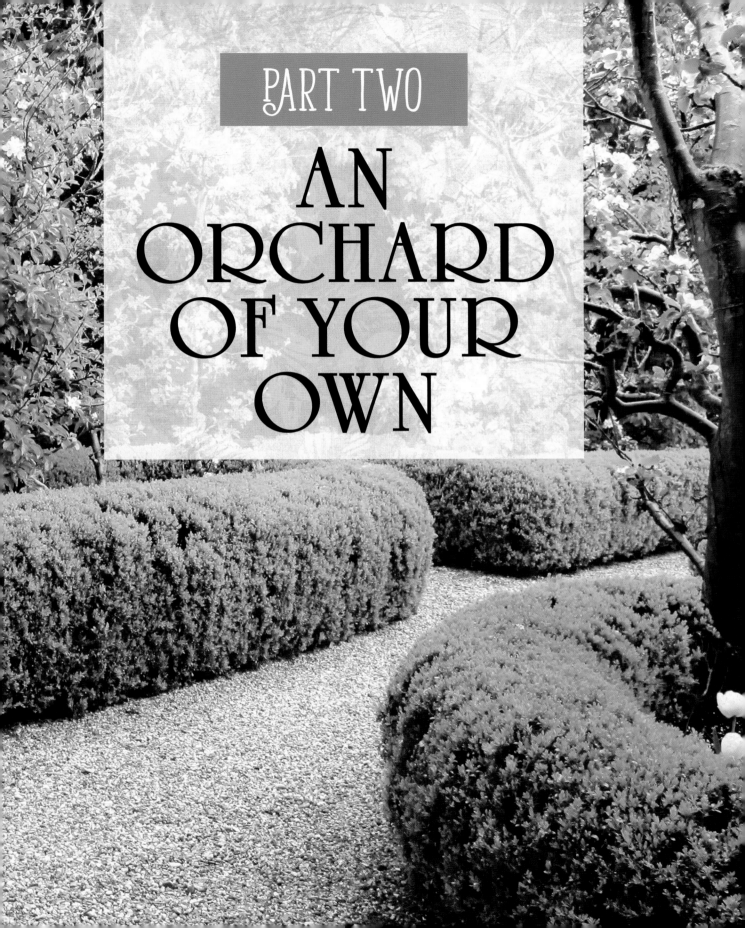

PART TWO

AN ORCHARD OF YOUR OWN

CHAPTER FIVE

CREATIVE ORCHARD DESIGN

In the first part of this book we explored the diversity and history of fruit trees and their place in our culture. This part looks at the more practical aspects of orchard living, including how to choose and take care of the trees. Yet just as important as the management of our trees is how we incorporate them into our lifestyle – ranging from the pleasures of cooking and eating to our desire to have our own piece of orchard heritage and to encourage wildlife. In addition, an orchard in any form can contribute to the garden aesthetic, our sense of well-being and sense of 'home'.

Elements of 'orchard' can be adopted whether a space is big or small (more on small spaces in the next chapter). And it is not just about the trees. The setting, design and the surrounding planting are key to integrating the orchard concept into our lives. It is what underpins the feel-good factor of fruit-growing and makes it possible and enjoyable in the long term.

This deck at the bottom of the garden is surrounded by fruit trees. There are trained specimens along the boundary behind it and apples against the picket fence to the left, while the lawn is punctuated with a damson, a pear and a Victoria plum – making the space secluded, but not overwhelmed.

Whether the orchard or potential orchard is in a domestic setting or in a space shared by the community, it can – must – be about more than productive growing. An orchard contributes to the garden aesthetic, our sense of well-being and sense of 'home'.

Furthermore, taking the orchard to the community (see Chapter 4) can create something idiosyncratic and meaningful to those who live there, perhaps offering more space to experiment and the chance to add larger trees to an urban tapestry. Community orchards and gardens are ahead of the curve here, and allotments are enjoying renewed popularity.

Whether the orchard or potential orchard is in a domestic setting or in a space shared by the community, it can – must – be about more than productive growing. Flowers and birds; elegant planters; lighting, seating and time spent thinking about the journey through the orchard and the vistas that emerge, all make an impact on our experience of the space.

Because the orchard is yours, the way it is organized has more to do with your tastes and gardening style than anything else. So this chapter is more about inspiration than about prescription. It shows ways in which the orchard concept has been embraced in spaces of all shapes and sizes. It is for you to take the ideas that appeal to you and adapt them to fit.

THE PLEASURE GARDEN

The idea of an orchard for pleasure is not new. In the Tudor period, kings and princes were the tastemakers, leaders of the land in more ways than one, and they thoroughly embraced

Ornamental orchards would often feature flowers for their beauty and perfume.

Grasses, dahlias and fondants of box surround the well in the centre of the formal walled garden at West Green House in Hampshire. Pairs of fruiting apple trees mark the entrance to each of the four paths that divide the lawn into quadrants, and frame the view to other areas of the garden.

the aesthetic. By the mid-sixteenth century, gardens belonging to aristocrats and royalty often included an ornamental orchard, rich in sensual symbolism and set around with scented plants, roses and hedging.

It was an era of fruity grandiosity. Fountains were de rigueur, and by 1531 the Privy Orchard at Hampton Court Palace was said to contain no fewer than seven sundials, together with heraldic animals such as horses and ante-lopes, greyhounds, lions and dragons. In the early seventeenth century, John Tradescant the elder stocked the grand new gardens at Hatfield House in Hertfordshire with exciting European plants, receiving hundreds of fruit trees from his counterpart in the French court.

As ideas from the Italian renaissance moved into French garden design, and from there on to Britain, further stylistic developments occ-urred and enthusiasm grew. Gardens became an exhibition of power, the pinnacle of which was Louis XIV's Potager du Roi at Versailles (see Chapter 1, page 34). In emulation and rivalry, magnificent gardens sprang up across Europe: Herrenhausen in Germany, Peterhof in Russia, Chatsworth in England and William of Orange's gardens – Het Loo in Holland and his baroque extravaganza at Hampton Court.

Water adds sparkle to gardens of all shapes and sizes.

This fashion persisted throughout the Tudor and Stuart period, gradually spreading to the minor nobility. Emulating Hatfield House might have been out of the question, but the modestly wealthy could easily incorporate elements of the grand pleasure orchards into their own gardens. A few cherry trees and a fountain, some beehives or a knot garden with some topiary, would demonstrate a nodding acquaintance with the style of the time. The more motivated might even go so far as to create an artificial hill or mount nearby, from which to survey all of which they were lord.

In 1618, the clergyman William Lawson published *A New Orchard and Pleasure Garden*, his sensible and lyrical descriptions encapsulating the spirit of the age. His paradise is "but a Garden and Orchard of trees and herbs, full of pleasures . . . and nothing there but delights". He reflects on an Elizabethan orchard with "an infinite variety of sweet smelling flowers . . . decking with sundry colours the green mantle of the earth", noting that red velvet damask roses, sweetly scented violets, music and long walkways are desirable, and the atmosphere of peace and calm to be savoured. Even the plundering birds are part of the delight. Of hearing blackbirds and thrushes singing on a May morning, he says, "I had rather want their company than my fruit."

Although a viewing mount and 500 cherry trees may be beyond reach for most of us, we can embrace the spirit of the gay, glorious pleasure orchards of the sixteenth century and create a world of tranquillity and fruitfulness; structure and scent. This multidimensional, sensual ideal elevates the worthy orchard to a place of joy or even frivolity. Like the kings of yore, we too can indulge in fragrant leisure and enjoyment of our gardens.

PARADISE GARDENS

Paradise gardens are of ancient Persian origin and generally consist of an enclosed space in which a formal garden is contained. The enclosures in which fruit trees were grown were known as *pairidaeza*, and this word gave rise to the Greek *paradeisos*. Paradise is, therefore, a secluded space of precious water, scents, fruit and flowers.

The gardens could be sumptuous – a heaven on earth for relaxation and pleasure. They harnessed sunlight, water and the cool shade within a pavilion. The canals and rills could be elaborate, and a tree with a spring issuing at its roots is a recurring symbol of eternal life.

This evocative image has been hugely influential on garden design, informing Islamic and European gardens, and feeding into Christianity as a version of the Garden of Eden. The word 'paradise' has an equivalent in a great number of languages, and the idea of a paradise garden appears in various forms in many countries, a good example being the Alhambra in Granada, Spain.

Although a paradise garden can be formal or relaxed in style, it is underpinned by a sense of earthly delight: of beauty and utility combined.

With its clean, crisp lines, reflective water and limited colour palette, this modern interpretation of a paradise garden at West Green House seems simple, but almost impossible. Yet the minute containers in which the frothy crab apple *Malus* 'Evereste' appears to be planted are deceptive: in fact, the roots are in the ground.

DESIGNING WITH FRUIT TREES

Fruit trees are highly adaptable in a garden design. Choose the right varieties and you can achieve an almost continuous show that starts with spring blossom, goes on to late-summer fruit and autumn colour, and then contributes structure to carry the display right through the winter.

There are peach trees with deep red leaves. In a good year, apples will produce clouds of blossom to rival the cherries in Tokyo. And if there is a corner that is crying out for spring blossom or autumn fireworks, but edible fruit is not a consideration, there is no shame in installing a crab apple such as *Malus tschonoskii*, with its firecracker hues, or M. 'Royal Beauty' (AGM), with dark pink flowers. The bees will still value it, and it will act as a good pollination partner for other trees in the neighbourhood.

Standard trees trained into pyramids or goblets can act as punctuation points within the design, injecting both height and energy, while free-standing espaliers or a colonnade of containers can create a see-through barrier that breaks a garden up into rooms or zones. (See Chapter 7 for details of trained fruit-tree forms.)

In diminutive gardens, small or narrow forms, either free-standing or in containers, can illuminate the space and add an all-important vertical dimension. Fruit trees also lend themselves to both formal and naturalistic treatments. In fact, it is quite unusual to see a garden fruit tree acting in a single design role – and those roles may have little, if anything, to do with the actual fruit.

Both ordinary fruit trees and crab apples can produce an impressive floral display.

Bring blossom indoors early in the year. Plums from the garden or hedgerow, glossy white pear blossom and the plump, rosy late-spring apple flowers are all gorgeous.

From a design or landscape-architecture point of view, it is important to maintain the space and retain the sense of 'orchard'. A feeling of permanence and peace is part of the charm.

ABOVE: Camping in an orchard filled with twinkling lights makes for a magical childhood experience.

LEFT: Like a living sculpture, the trunk of this mature quince tree has a wonderful movement and texture.

An old orchard made new

Design is often thought about in the context of small spaces and in relation to buildings. But this is not always a good fit if one has a larger garden or smallholding, for example. When tasked with rejuvenating a traditional local orchard, or if you are lucky enough to have an acre of semi-derelict trees to play with, a broader approach is called for.

From a design or landscape-architecture point of view, it is important to maintain the space and retain the sense of 'orchard'. A sense of permanence and

Include plenty of places to sit, at different times of day and in different weather.

peace is part of the charm. But it is also desirable to consider how it might now be used. If it was once a farm orchard and is now part of a garden or a communal area, people may want to use it in new and different ways.

Some of these will be practical: is there good access for a mower? Is there somewhere dry to sit? Are the old trees safe? Would new planting rejuvenate the area?

Making an older orchard somewhere pleasant and functional is relatively simple. Maintain the trees and mow the grass regularly. Seating is always a

bonus, and if the orchard is going to be used for parties or events, or somewhere that children can camp during summer weekends, it might be worth thinking about a weather-proof power point and outside tap. A fire pit surrounded by logs to sit on is a nice focal point.

Equally, while maintaining and restoring the trees, it is perfectly reasonable to update the sense of the place so that you can live with it, and in it, happily and comfortably. Opening up a vista, planting an avenue of trees or reiterating the old orchard as a largely lifestyle space, with mown paths, elegant benches, idly rambling roses and bursts of spring colour, may be what makes you happy.

A new lifestyle orchard

The great thing about starting a garden or an orchard from scratch is that you are not limited by the existing plants. There are no old trees to be accommodated, and you can choose the ultimate size of the varieties you fancy.

It pays, however, to think carefully about the space. Draw a plan of how the different elements will fit together – how much space the trees will take up, where the hard landscaping will go, and the position of other feature plants. Also draw an elevation (view from the front), so you can see which vistas will be created by the trees and which eyesores will be hidden. The easiest way to do this is to print out a photograph and draw on it.

The twenty-first-century pleasure garden can contain all the lovely things that were enjoyed in the sixteenth century: seating and music; scent and birdsong. But it can also come with all mod cons. For example, think about lighting and power: fairy lights and uplighters can be wired in early on, or you could use

Pretty arches, trellis and obelisks, and site-specific sculpture can make your orchard personal.

Little details add an element of surprise.

In smart pots and underplanted with herbs, these handsome olive trees make a bold statement.

solar-powered lights and hang candle lanterns on the branches of your trees.

Don't overlook opportunities for entertaining and outdoor dining spaces. A fire pit, barbecue or chiminea could feature, as could other delightful details: ornaments, artworks, containers or trellis.

Fruit trees and the formal garden

Formal gardens are balanced and symmetrical and are usually based on geometric shapes, such as a rectangle with repeated squares or diamonds. Even when the garden or borders are curved, formality can be injected with repeated elements and shapes, or a bold single theme, for a tranquil and ordered effect.

Within the formal garden, fruit trees can perform a range of roles:

❋ They can be trained flat as a background to other planting, effectively as formal hedging.

❋ They can be trained to a low level, acting as edging for a border or path without creating a visual barrier.

✳ Pruned with a clear trunk and with the canopy at a high level, they can have the effect of a visual exclamation mark or full stop, or of creating a high continuous screen to look through or under.

✳ Fruit trees are often used as specimens, pruned and trained into a geometric or regular form. These can be either planted in the ground or in containers that inject a solidity or block of colour. The trees might also be pleached (the branches interwoven).

✳ The simplest way to get a sense of formality is to repeat themes or patterns, such as plant varieties or forms as pairs or repeated pairs.

ABOVE: The formal edible garden at Villandry, France. The ideas of trained fruit around borders and specimen trees can be adopted on a much more modest scale.

BELOW: Clipped box and tulips add crispness to the soft apple blossom at West Green House, Hampshire.

PLANTING COMBINATIONS

The task of managing fruit trees in combination with other plants covers everything from remembering to mow the surrounding grass to incorporating the trees into a herbaceous border. Being permanent and, in general, large plants, fruit trees have a diverse supporting role to play, as well as being significant performers in their own right.

When it comes to planting combinations, orchard design can be interpreted in myriad ways. Arguably the most popular (and lowest maintenance) option is a cultivated wilderness, where semi-native grassland is augmented with bulbs and punctuated by mown paths. But more formal arrangements are possible, where the orchard represents a fairly tightly managed section of a larger garden and its visual impact is part of a greater whole.

Underplanting and the cultivated wilderness

An orchard rising above a swathe of meadow blooms is a wonderful sight. And, while this can be managed relatively easily with native flower species, it can also be augmented with ornamentals and bulbs. Blossom trees can be underplanted with a series of spring bulbs, starting with snowdrops and dwarf narcissi and finishing with a crescendo of tulips.

TOP RIGHT: Spring bulbs can provide an early splash of colour.

BOTTOM RIGHT: A river of white narcissi with pear and plum blossom brings together all the freshness of spring.

ABOVE: These fat green apples look rather handsome, suspended above a relaxed late-summer border of alstroemeria, phlox and hydrangeas.

TOP: In spring, the orchard floor at Canons Ashby in Northamptonshire is frothy with cow parsley and the blue spires of camassia.

Unless the orchard is for decorative or wildlife purposes only, however, it is a good idea to ensure that the bulbs and blooms are out of the way at the time you want to pick the fruit and prune the trees in autumn and winter.

Back-of-border trees

Older trees often find themselves incorporated in the back of the border, having been there for some time before the present garden was created. This can look rather nice, as the fruit cascades over the herbaceous and shrub planting in an informal mash-up of practical and decorative purpose.

Occasionally the older trees bring something else to the party. Old espalier hedges, for example, sometimes persist in older gardens, as a formal backdrop to the more ephemeral and lively seasonal planting.

Fruit trees as structure and infrastructure

While it is easy to assume that trees are always the dominant feature in the landscape or garden, in many seasons they are not really the main event at all.

They can have a quite literal supporting role, clothed in climbers such as clematis or roses. They can also play a part in edging a path or border or framing a view, or in some other structural or ornamental capacity as a coherent part of the planting scheme.

TOP: The gnarly wood of this former espalier hedge is a contrast to the tightly pruned foliage. It makes a solid backdrop to the changing floral display of summer.

RIGHT: This walnut tree at Les Jardins de Roquelin is covered in cascading climbing roses.

The angular, moss-clad branches of this crackled old crone of a tree bring drama and energy to the still winter scene.

Silhouetted by the rising sun, the walnut tree dominates the frosty, empty vegetable garden.

THE WINTER GARDEN

Once their leaves fall, trees lay aside their bouncy, rounded summer persona to become something far more stark and dramatic. The trees become watchful; nature a little more raw. Older apples and pears develop knobbly elbows and witch-fingers that stretch out to catch passers-by; the tangled crown of rattling twigs suddenly unkempt and atavistic.

The raw energy of an aged standard specimen is particularly striking, but espaliers and other trained forms also add heft, structure and a sense of continuity to the winter garden.

ABOVE: The wide border that surrounds the main lawn at West Green House is punctuated with a series of multi-stem crab-apple trees. They are pruned to a clear stem of around 2m (6'6"), over which hangs a tight canopy. Thus, at eye level, they frame the views across to the knot of clipped box and eating apples in the centre of the walled garden.

TOP RIGHT: At the Chaumont-sur-Loire International Garden Festival in 2014 the theme was 'Seven Deadly Sins'. Since *pêcher* is French for a peach tree and *péché* means sin, this garden was created around a punning representation of a peach tree with a subtext meditation on sensuality.

BOTTOM RIGHT: Art does not have to be classical. At Château du Rivau is usually modern and rather unexpected!

SCULPTURE IN THE ORCHARD

Sculpture can draw the eye and provide something interesting to look at when the garden is bare. The choice, as with other design elements, is a matter of taste. Classical sculptures work well in a garden setting, while something more abstract or modern can be a good contrast to a naturalistic orchard wilderness. Decorating a garden with *objets trouvés* can add an idiosyncratic personal touch.

In a small garden orchard, trees trained against the walls are not only an effective use of space but can also be, in themselves, sculptural.

ABOVE: The brutalist architecture of the South Bank Centre in London is plenty strong enough to take large potted trees, but before you start loading up your own roof with foliage and compost, make sure it is sufficiently robust.

LEFT: Growing fruit and veg in containers means that a productive garden can be achieved in the smallest of urban courtyards.

OPPOSITE: Tucked up in the conservatory, a citrus tree and buckets of herbs need not fear a late frost.

THE CONTAINER FRUIT GARDEN

For the purposes of small and urban garden design, planting trees in containers has distinct advantages. It enables an elegant and flexible use of space that can incorporate many, if not all, of the design elements discussed so far – including putting your orchard where you can see it. The trees can be seasonal and structural, they could be formal, and they can work alone or with other ornamentals. And the best thing is that if you move house you can take the garden with you.

With the flexibility to move trees around the garden and reconfigure them at will,

the modern orchard gardener can create different tableaux and bring individual trees to the fore at their peak. The approach also opens up possibilities for mini-orchards on balconies and terraces and in roof gardens.

The fruit trees can be combined in a group with tubs of seasonal flowers, shrubs and grasses, and other containerized trees. With care, they can also be directly underplanted with annuals or bulbs. See Chapter 6 (pages 158-60) for more about fruit trees in containers and in small spaces.

Roses take the stage after apple blossom fades.

ORCHARD DESIGN IDEAS

Here are some pick-and-mix ideas for orchard gardens of all sizes. Many of these ideas are discussed earlier in this chapter, while the suggestions for small-scale planting combinations are a springboard for inspiration.

❋ Plant young trees in formal lines or squares. Surround them with clipped evergreens.

❋ Create avenues with a focal point – this could be a sculpture, a building, a large tree of a different species or a wall-trained fruit tree.

❋ Grow climbers such as roses up the larger trees (ensuring that the climber won't overwhelm its support).

❋ Introduce fragrant plants. Edge borders with rosemary or lavender; cluster winter-flowering honeysuckle (*Lonicera fragrantissima*) or *Sarcococca* species around the bare winter stems, and create a sea of scented narcissi.

❋ Use plants that will provide a pop of colour or texture in the dark winter days. Trees with persistent fruit work really hard, and these can be backed up by brightly coloured dogwood (*Cornus* spp.) stems, underplanted with late-autumn-, winter- or early-spring-flowering bulbs.

❋ Play with concepts and words – of apples, pears, and so on. Create visual puns or a themed walk.

❋ Create a tree-house-style viewing platform in a nearby tree, ascended by sturdy steps, or think about the view of your orchard from upstairs in the house.

❋ Add sheep or chickens to the theme; if you don't want real ones, then wicker models are effective.

❋ Think about using fences and gates to enhance the scene. Don't forget seating, and what about abstract sculpture?

❋ Personalize the space. Be creative! Play on a theme, such as Alice in Wonderland or showjumping (creating jumps out of espaliers and uprights); add fairy doors, or string lights or bunting between the trees. Punk the idea: anything goes. Genteel pleasure gardens and crazy, enthusiastic, fruit-themed mash-ups are both perfectly acceptable. Why do it the usual way just because other people do?

TOP LEFT: Trained fruit forms a bower for this viewing seat at Jardin du Plessis Sasnières in the Loire Valley. BOTTOM LEFT: Plant a low hedge with fragrant French lavender. TOP RIGHT: All the aesthetic benefits of domestic animals; none of the risk of them eating your plants! BOTTOM RIGHT: In this microscopic formal potager, the focal fruit tree is underplanted with mint and chives and scaled by black-eyed Susan (*Thunbergia*). Plums are trained along rope swags for edging. This idea could be used for any strip of garden with a good path.

CHAPTER SIX

FRUIT TREES FOR EVERY SPACE

While gracious collections of fruit trees have long been a feature of large suburban gardens and grand country estates, you don't actually need acres of land to have a viable and productive orchard. Small spaces offer the opportunity to be creative with the orchard concept – if we update and repurpose it to fit into the ways that we now live.

Using the conservation definition of an orchard as 'a minimum of five fruit or nut trees' (as described in Chapter 2), the smallest, most ordinary back garden suddenly has plenty of space. A roof terrace or even a decent balcony can welcome a containerized micro-orchard. And, with a little invention and imagination, the gardener can elevate the mundane into an art form.

This chapter is about how fruit trees may be used in spaces of different sizes. It describes how they can contribute to garden design, and why your choice of tree is a very personal one. As tastes and locations are individual, it also considers the general factors that will help you make the right decisions when selecting your new tree.

The private courtyard outside West Green House in Hampshire has an orchard of apple trees surrounded by box 'doughnuts'.

The second half of this chapter deals with the nitty-gritty of choosing fruit trees: the timings of the crop and size of the tree, for example. It discusses rootstocks and pollination partners, which are particularly relevant to working with limited space.

Paradoxically, planting and conservation regulations may be introducing orchards into urban gardens and streets by stealth. In some urban conservation areas in the UK, restrictions are placed upon cutting back or felling trees, unless it is a fruit tree. So people in towns may be opting for fruit trees in order to be able to manage them without applying to the council first. Thus, conservation policy may be unwittingly exerting a pressure in favour of urban orchards.

YOUR GARDEN, YOUR ORCHARD

There are so many different ways of growing fruit, and so many fruits to choose from, that almost anyone can accommodate an orchard. This could be single-species or a mix of favourites: apples, pears, plums and greengages are both beautiful and flavoursome. With favourable growing conditions, your orchard could also include exotica such as olives, lemons, limes, apricots or peaches, or climbers such as kiwis – while more unusual and striking species such as Chilean guava or Szechuan pepper are surprisingly hardy. On the domestic level, what is important are your tastes, culture and interests. Grow the things you like (to look at and to eat). Experiment with what interests and excites you.

ABOVE: While kiwi fruit don't actually grow on trees, they make an attractive addition to the garden.

TOP: Chilean guava is a compact bush with pretty pink bell-flowers; its blueberry-like fruit taste a bit like strawberries. It grows surprisingly well in the UK.

OPPOSITE: This tiny urban garden has citrus trees on the patio and trained fruit around its minute veg plot.

The smallest productive area can boast a few diminutive trees.

FRUIT IN VERY SMALL SPACES

While you may not be able to magic up a bigger garden, you can choose smaller trees. It is quite possible to have an orchard of five trees, or even more, if they are grafted on to very dwarfing rootstocks (see pages 165-7) or are formally trained to take up less space, perhaps as a narrow column or flat against a wall or a wire.

Making a micro-orchard on a roof terrace, balcony or courtyard has the huge advantage that the trees are very close to where we spend most of our time. It is the orchard equivalent of a pot of herbs on the windowsill:

convenient, near to hand and every bit as achievable. Just outside the window is a cool, green world of productivity – and the prize a slice of lemon for a gin and tonic, or the makings of the most locally sourced tarte Tatin you'll ever eat.

Here, the range of plants that you are able to grow may also be extended by the local microclimate, since cities tend to be warmer than the surrounding countryside, due to the mass of buildings acting as a giant storage heater. It is no coincidence that the largest outdoor fruiting olive tree in Britain can be found in the middle of London, in the walled Chelsea Physic Garden and next to the River Thames: all features which raise and stabilize local temperatures in winter.

Trained fruit trees can take up much less space than standard trees.

Szechuan pepper is hardy and striking. The leaves are edible, and the berries feature in Chinese five spice.

Container gardening with tree fruit

Assuming that your tree is small enough and your pot is large enough, there is no problem with growing fruit trees in containers – and it can be particularly helpful in small gardens, as it keeps the tree more compact than if it were grown in the open ground.

Trees come in various sizes, and the ultimate size depends upon both the tree itself and the rootstock on to which it has been grafted (see pages 165-7). The important thing is to choose a plant that, when fully grown, won't be too large for its allocated space. Fruit trees in pots do best in a sheltered situation, where their roots won't be damaged by wind-rock. And,

on a balcony, deck or roof terrace, remember to check that the structure is robust enough to take the weight of the trees – and any surrounding planting – together with all those pots of damp soil.

Exposure may be an issue with roof gardens and balconies, with the wind drying the leaves like so much wet washing and roughly buffeting delicate branches. A tree in leaf also has a not-inconsiderable wind resistance. You don't want to see your plants flying past your window into the street below, and horizontal is not a good look.

But another bonus of growing small trees in permanent containers is that you can experiment with species that may be tender or

FAMILY TREES AND TINY TREES

If space is tight, 'family trees' are available, where different types of fruit are grafted on to a single rootstock. You then get a plant that can yield both cooking and eating apples, or pears that ripen at different times. These are often marketed as being the ultimate in versatility, but in fact there is the risk that one variety will come to dominate the rest. Care must be taken in choosing the right varieties, and it takes a certain amount of skill to keep them in balance.

With an increased consumer enthusiasm for grow-your-own and fruit in small spaces, tree nurseries have responded by making truly dwarf trees available. At around 1.5m (5'), they may be small but they can be amazingly productive. All of the usual suspects – apples, pears, plums and cherries – are available in this form, together with more unusual specimens, if you look in the right place (see Resources for suppliers). And, with the micro-orchard gardener in mind, the very small trees tend to be self-fertile, allowing a potted orchard of enormous variety.

Fruit breeders have an eye to what both looks and tastes good. Bred by Lubera, this dwarf peach has pretty red leaves and maroon fruit.

require winter protection. Citrus such as lemons and kumquats can be grown outside in summer and brought into a greenhouse or a cool, bright room to overwinter. Dormant peaches likewise can spend winter in the greenhouse, or, since they don't need light, in an airy shed, until the buds break and all risk of frost is past.

See Chapter 7, page 183, for more about caring for fruit trees in permanent containers.

An ornamental cherry is the backdrop to a deck which has several trained fruit trees behind it and looks out on to a fruit lawn. Yet the dominant impression is not 'orchard'.

SPECIMEN TREES AND TRAINED FORMS

A tree which has good blossom and autumn colour can look great as a focal point in a veg patch or lawn, or integrated into a small garden orchard. Planted in open soil, it will need less watering and feeding than its containerized brethren and, if desired, a bigger specimen can be used.

But just because a tree is a permanent and static structure does not mean that is has to be a dominant feature. There are many gardens that use trained fruit to edge a path or potager, for example. Espaliers on wires can provide a backdrop to a border, and will maintain both height and structure during the winter months. Columnar forms of cherry or apple will produce a tall, narrow vertical, which can act as an accent plant in herbaceous planting.

A fruit hedge works well either side of a path here at Greys Court, Oxfordshire.

Tall, narrow trees, like the cherry to the right of this picture, provide height and punctuation in a rambunctious herbaceous border.

Trained specimens with multiple stems can also perform a range of design roles – adding height, structure or unusual interest, and framing or screening other parts of the garden. If the aim is to invoke the five-trees rule for a small garden orchard, a mix-and-match collection of fruit in containers and in the ground; of trained fruit, dwarf fruit and half standards, can rapidly tick all the boxes. (See pages 168 and 171-3 for details of fruit-tree forms.)

CHOOSING YOUR FRUIT TREE

Unless you have unlimited space, time and budget, not to mention a collector's mentality, the chances are that your tree will have to work for its living and its place in your orchard, possibly performing several roles at once.

What it actually has to do depends on the sort of gardener you are and your personal tastes. Perhaps what matters to you is produce, to cook with or to eat fresh. Maybe the priority is looks: the structure and blossom, the colour of the autumn leaves and the visual impact of the ripening fruit. How will you reconcile the needs of the tree – and its innate nature – with what you want it for? When you are choosing a tree, you need to think about what it will look like, how big it will get, what the fruit will taste like and when it will appear.

The rest of this chapter explains the things that you need to know when choosing the right tree for the space you have, whether large or small. The minutiae of rootstocks and pollination partners can seem a little esoteric, but it is actually pretty straightforward. And, with the benefit of some research and careful thought about your own requirements, you won't have unreasonable expectations of what your tree will or won't do.

It is also important to understand the local conditions in your growing space, and what you can do to make sure that your tree goes in a spot where it will survive and thrive. This is covered in the next chapter.

Appearance, taste and timing

Fruit trees are highly variable. They can look distinctly different from species to species and within species. The choice of rootstock makes the same tree available in a range of sizes, and there are also different forms: tall and thin or small and round; compact or imposing; naturalistic or formally trained. Formal, naturalistic and cottage gardens all

Gardens are all about love.

have room for fruit trees. But you'll never get a Bramley to grow into a neat column, or a standard to stay small enough for its patio pot, so it saves a lot of trouble if you get the right thing first time.

The question of taste is another matter. It is highly subjective, based on personal responses to flavour, scent and memory and the things that spark hunger or comfort. Preference boils down to the individual palate, which depends also on habits, culture and experience. One man's arboreal delight is another man's compost fodder.

Tastes can be capricious. Bramley is marvellous, but the fat, yellow cooking apple at the bottom of my orchard has a fragrance that transcends time. My favourite eating apple changes each year (it was Devonshire Quarrenden, then Lord Lambourne, then Claygate

Damsons make a sublimely tart jam, but they, and gages, are often ignored in the face of Victoria plums.

The delicious Claygate Pearmain.

Pearmain and is currently Cornish Aromatic, if you were wondering).

Then there is the question of how long you are prepared to wait for results. Some varieties crop sooner than others, and dwarf trees will usually fruit sooner than standards (see pages 168-9 for details). You may prefer to sacrifice height to get speedy returns – or maybe a series of small trees in a teeny orchard may be exactly what you are after.

If the question 'when?' is more about what time in the season than what time this decade: the cherries start in high summer, while apples ripen from late summer right through to late autumn – some keeping until mid-spring (see Chapter 8 for details about storage). If you want to get a quart out of a pint pot, look at family trees (see box on page 160).

The fruit tree you buy has to be the one whose fruit you want to eat (or drink), or at the very least look at. Subject to a bit of common sense, there are no wrong answers. Make a sensible choice for the space and location you have, and in return your tree will continue to deliver delightful gifts on a regular basis, while pleasing you with its form and colour. Thus the two of you will have a long and happy affiliation.

UNDERSTANDING FRUIT TREES

To make an informed choice about what will work best in a given set of gardening conditions, taking into consideration both space and design, there are a number of things to bear in

The fruit tree you buy has to be the one whose fruit you want to eat (or drink), or at the very least look at. Subject to a bit of common sense, there are no wrong answers.

mind. This section covers the main types of fruit and how they tick, focusing on apple trees as an example. Where other species vary significantly, this is indicated in the text.

Grafts and rootstocks

There are thousands of different apple varieties, of different flavours, sizes and growth habits. But plant a pip from any one and you'll end up with something completely other, because a seed contains genes from two different parents. This can result in exciting new varieties, but it's more probable that the resulting fruit will be less than the sum of its component parts. You also won't have any control over how big the tree gets.

To get a named variety, the desired fruit is propagated vegetatively by grafting a scion from the parent plant on to a rootstock. Basically, you take a cutting from the tree you want and attach it to the roots of another tree that has been chosen to behave in a certain way. This controls the end result.

The topwood – the apple variety you get when it fruits – will retain its usual shape and form, but the rootstock heavily influences the ultimate size of the tree. While some apples, such

as Sunset and Bountiful, are naturally modest in size, Bramley's Seedling is a whopper.

A rootstock can moderate or enhance a tree's natural vigour and, depending on the type of rootstock chosen, means that a variety may be available in small, medium or large. (See box on pages 166-7 for details of rootstocks for different trees.) Most commercially available fruit trees are grafted on to a type of rootstock

Where the rootstock and scion have been joined with a whip-and-tongue graft on this walnut tree, a scar is clearly visible. Even when it is less obvious, the graft is usually identifiable as a knobbly section on the stem.

called MM106, known as a semi-dwarfing rootstock – which should be indicated on the label when the tree is sold. This semi-dwarfing (or semi-vigorous) rootstock produces a kind of catch-all, medium-sized tree.

Grafting is a good way to propagate cherished trees or old varieties. Local orchard groups and some gardens run grafting courses – see the RHS, National Trust or The Urban Orchard Project for ideas.

For general retailers, 'kind of medium-sized' works well. The market for the great big standard trees of yore is limited, especially in urban areas. And, while increasingly popular, trained fruit and very small trees are still a slightly specialist area. However, certain suppliers (see Resources) sell trees on a variety of rootstocks and may graft your favourite tree on to the rootstock of your choice.

In a traditional, grazed orchard, large standard trees are usual, although (if you are lucky enough to have a decent area to plant up) you can get away with half standards, which are easier to pick. When the trees are mature, you can still walk between and beneath them and, although not small, they are a more manageable size if you are trying to incorporate a decent collection of regional or heritage cultivars into an urban space, for example.

At the other end of the scale, it is worth noting that trees on dwarfing rootstocks need mollycoddling. They stay smaller because the rootstock is incompetent. As a result, they need good, rich soil and plenty of water, and they must be staked to prevent them blowing over. If your conditions are not great, it is worth choosing something a little more vigorous.

TYPES OF ROOTSTOCK

For **apples**, there are five types of rootstock:

* **M27** Extremely dwarfing; grows into a very small tree or bush, 1.5-1.8m (5-6') high.
* **M9** Very dwarfing; creates a tree 2.5-3m (8-10') high.
* **M26** Dwarfing; similar to M9 but a bit more vigorous, 3-3.5m (10'-11'6") high.
* **MM106** Semi-dwarfing or semi-vigorous. This is the average tree, suiting the majority of gardens and is widely available; grows to 4-5m (13-16').
* **MM111 and M25** Vigorous rootstocks that will produce a large, standard tree, up to 7.5m (25') tall.

Pears were traditionally grafted on to wild pear rootstocks, but most are now grafted on to quince:

* **Quince C** is a moderately vigorous rootstock, producing a tree 3.5-4m (11'6"-13') tall.
* **Quince A** is slightly more vigorous, producing trees of ultimate height 4-4.5m (13'-14'6").
* **Pyrodwarf** gives a similar size to Quince A, but the tree fruits earlier and is more tolerant of dry and chalky soils.
* **Wild pear** is the traditional, highly vigorous solution, reaching a height of 10-15m (33-49'). The spread can vary considerably, depending on the variety.

Grafting a damson on to a St Julien A rootstock will produce a medium-sized tree.

The Colt rootstock will create a cherry tree that is garden-sized rather than forest-sized.

Some varieties of **plums** can be propagated via their suckering shoots. Now they are usually grafted on to dwarfing **Pixy** rootstocks, producing trees 2.5-3.5m (8'-11'6") tall, or the semi-vigorous **St Julien A**, which produces trees of about 3.5-4.5m (11'6"-4'6").

Historically, **cherries** were grafted on to wild cherry roots, which grew into enormous orchard trees. Now garden cherries are grown on **Gisela 5** rootstocks, producing trees that are only 2.5-3m (8-10') tall, or the semi-dwarfing **Colt** rootstocks, which grow to 3.5-4.5m (11'6"-14'6") tall.

Peaches, nectarines and apricots use the same rootstocks as plums. But new developments with rootstocks such as **Montclaire** for peaches and nectarines, and **Torinel** for apricots, make for trees that are slightly smaller than their pre-decessors and are hardier and more productive, respectively.

Figs are grown on their own roots.

Quinces are grown on wild pear or quince rootstocks.

Mulberries are grown either from cuttings or on the rootstock of a white mulberry to promote earlier cropping.

Medlars are grown on the rootstocks of quince or hawthorn, which will produce a small tree, or on wild pear rootstocks, which will produce a large tree.

The different rootstocks confer other benefits and disadvantages beyond moderating the ultimate height of a tree. They can influence the hardiness of the tree and the preference for different soil conditions, for example (see note opposite about dwarfing rootstocks).

Fruit tree classifications

Fruit trees can be bought or pruned into a range of types, shapes and sizes:

⁕ **Maiden (or maiden whip)** A 1-year-old tree on a single stem. The size varies according to fruit type and rootstock. Bought bare-root, this is the cheapest way to acquire trees.

⁕ **Feathered maiden** A 1-year-old tree that has naturally developed some branches without pruning. It can be pruned to any shape and may be a little more expensive than a maiden whip.

⁕ **Bush** A tree that is 2 or 3 years old and usually on one of the less vigorous rootstocks. It has been pruned to create a head of three or four branches above a 1m (3') trunk.

⁕ **Half standard** A tree grafted on to a semi-vigorous rootstock, with a clear trunk about 1.2-1.5m (4-5') and a head of branches.

⁕ **Standard** A tree on a vigorous rootstock with a clear stem of 1.8m (6') and a head of branches.

Cropping

The younger the tree you buy, the longer it will take to crop. A maiden, which is a 1-year-old grafted tree, will take about 5 years before it produces much fruit, although some varieties naturally crop sooner in their lives and others very much later. Those that crop early are known as 'precocious', and include the apples Braeburn, Granny Smith and Red Delicious, and Conference pears. The opposite of precocious – naturally slow to bear fruit – is 'reluctant'.

The bigger the tree will be, the longer it takes to produce fruit. The more dwarfing the rootstock, the more precocious the crop.

Once fruiting is established, not all trees will crop every year. Some are pretty reliable, but others are more occasional or establish a biennial cropping pattern, where they fruit heavily one year and take the following year off. Fruiting can also be inhibited by poor care or circumstance, for example by not feeding the tree, accidentally cutting the flower buds off when pruning, late frost, drought or poor choice of location.

To a certain extent a tree will regulate itself. The mass of blossom in spring will not all convert to fruit. Some flowers may remain unfertilized, and the tree also undergoes a process of natural thinning called the June

Fruits often thin themselves in the June Drop. But when pollination is very good, the fruitlets often need further thinning so that the tree is not overburdened and the remaining fruit will reach a good size.

Drop, whereby some of the fertilized fruits fail to develop and fall off, the remainder growing bigger and plumper as a result. This process also reduces the risk of the crop becoming so heavy that it literally tears the tree apart – a particular risk with plums.

Pollination

Not long ago, I showed a chap around my orchard as he reminisced about the apple trees that were in his garden when he was a child, and the wonderful fruit that they had produced. "But one of them died and then the other stopped fruiting, so my dad cut it down in the end," he finished, rather sadly.

The thing about apple trees is that they are usually not, or not very, self-fertile. To get fruit they need a pollination partner – another compatible tree that flowers at around the same time to fertilize the seeds. If there are lots of trees in the area then this is less of an issue, but if there are few then it should definitely be borne in mind. If I could turn back the clock, I would advise my visitor's father, amongst several other possible remedies, to plant a new pollination partner rather than cutting down the unproductive tree.

However, once you have your trees and their pollination partners in place, it can be a distinct advantage to grow them in a small space. It is generally recommended to plant apples not more than 100m (330') apart, and this requirement is easily met in a town garden or on a roof terrace. As the bee flies, such a modern orchard is buffet dining, and pollen will be spread merrily from plant to plant.

Once fertilization has taken place, the flower dies back and the fruit and seeds begin to form. Although each seed is a genetically unique combination of the two parents, the fruit will always be 'right' for the mother-tree it grows on. So, whatever pollinates a Sunset apple tree, the tree will produce Sunset fruit. If the Sunset pollinates a different variety of tree, the apple that forms as a result will not resemble its paternal Sunset.

Apple pollination groups

Apple varieties are divided into groups according to when they flower. Most simply, these are early flowering, mid-season flowering, mid-season to late flowering, and late flowering; the groups are often numbered, from early to late. The ideal pollination partner is a

A pollination partner is another variety that flowers at about the same time. This Falstaff apple is in pollination group 3. It is self-fertile, but cropping is improved if it cross-pollinates with an apple in groups 2, 3 or 4.

tree in the same group, or, failing that, in the one immediately before or after (above or below in the numbering). An early-flowering apple will not pollinate a late-flowering apple, simply because they are not at the same stage at the same time.

There is an additional challenge to apple pollination, in that some varieties are triploid: they have an extra set of chromosomes. This tends to produce vigorous trees, but it also means that, although perfectly fertile on the fruit-bearing female side, they produce very poor pollen. So to grow these apples successfully you need two pollination partners, providing pollen both for the triploid apple and for each other. Triploid apples include Blenheim Orange, Crispin, Ashmead's Kernel, Bramley's Seedling and Jupiter.

As long as they are in flower at the same time, the apples don't much care whether their partner is a domestic cultivar or a cider or crab apple. In fact, crab apples are a particularly good thing! They produce a profusion of blossom over a long period and are usually genetically compatible with other varieties, ideal to interplant amongst the fruit crop and an aesthetic asset to boot.

Pollination groups and partners are listed in good fruit catalogues, and also on the RHS and Orange Pippin websites (see Resources).

Pollination in other fruit

A tree's pollination needs vary according to variety in other fruit too:

❊ **Pears** follow the same pollination pattern as apples. Similarly divided into groups, they

The petals fall from the cherry blossom as the fruit starts to swell.

too need to be planted near a compatible pollination partner. Conference is self-fertile but it crops better with a partner.

❊ **Peaches, apricots and nectarines** are invariably self-fertile.

❊ **Plums** mostly need cross-pollination and, as with apples and pears, there are several pollination groups. Certain dessert varieties, such as Victoria and Opal, are self-fertile.

❊ **Figs** tend to be self-fertile.

❊ Some **cherries** – Lapins, Sunburst, Stella and Morello – are self-fertile. Others are more complicated and may require a specific (usually named) pollination partner.

THE POLLINATORS

Fruit trees are insect-pollinated, and they are a good source of nectar for bees and hoverflies. A healthy local population of pollinators will improve fruit-cropping, but there is concern that beneficial insects are in decline.

Providing habitat and additional nectar sources for insects, before and after the season that the fruit trees flower, will give them a boost. Once a tree is established, it can be surrounded with wildflowers, bulbs or other nectar-rich ornamentals such as sedums, borage, lavender or echinacea.

Feed the bees, and they will pollinate your fruit.

Trained fruit trees

The good thing about fruit trained into restricted forms (for example, espaliers) is that it is, in effect, two-dimensional. The trees can be wide or tall, but, because their shape is very shallow, their encroachment into the garden is minimal – ideal if the aim is to make the best use of space and to maximize productivity. It also allows the tree to add a decorative, structural element to the garden, whether in fruit, in flower or in sculptural winter nudity.

The easiest approach is to buy your tree already trained. It may be a little more expensive, but the hard work is already done and you will just need to plant, maintain and enjoy it. Restricted trained forms are spur-fruiting varieties (see box on page 172), and the idea is to create a branch with fruit spread evenly along the length, rather than just at the end.

There are many ways of training and restricting fruit-tree growth, but the three most common forms are the espalier, the fan and the cordon.

✳ **Espaliers** Suitable for apples and pears rather than stone fruit, these can be free-standing or wall-trained. Pairs of branches are pruned to form tiers, and trained along a horizontal wire either side of a vertical trunk. The

The apples on this espalier hang like baubles on a Christmas tree.

SPUR-FRUITING AND TIP-FRUITING

Apples and pears are either spur-fruiting or tip-fruiting, which means that they produce fruit either from flowers borne on the knobbly spurs along the length of the branch, or from flowers borne mostly at the tips of the branches. Tip-bearers are not suitable for training into restricted forms.

If you are in any doubt, take a good look at the tree. Whereas leaf buds are small and lie flat against the branch, flower buds are larger, plumper and more prominent.

When these stepover trees get a little bigger, they will divide the vegetable border into neat geometric shapes.

tiers are spaced about 40cm (1'4") apart. A 'stepover' is a single-tiered espalier, forming a T-shape about 30-40cm (1'-1'4") high.

※ **Fans** These trees have branches that radiate from a low central point. Horizontal wires are fixed, usually to a wall, and the fan of branches is trained across them. This is a technique frequently used for peaches, apricots, cherries, plums and also figs, which benefit from the extra warmth absorbed by, and radiated from, the wall.

※ **Cordons** Most cordons are single stems, with fruiting spurs along the length. If they are grown diagonally against a wall, they are an extremely efficient use of the area available, as the angle allows for a longer stem than if they were vertical. Using cordons rather than a single fan-trained tree or espalier means that you can have lots of adjacent varieties in a relatively small space. The sloping angle also encourages fruiting rather than growth.

There are other forms of cordon, including a system of two vertical stems trained into a U-shape from a short trunk. This is an excellent use of space on a narrow wall – by a door, for example.

CHAPTER SEVEN

TREE PLANTING AND CARE

All trees need certain things. They all require water, light, nutrients and room to grow, and they vary in their tolerance to adverse conditions. Most will benefit from formative pruning, which is pruning when young to maintain an attractive and balanced shape, and maintenance pruning, to maximize the amount of wood that will bear fruit.

This chapter explains how to help your trees thrive. It asks you to think about your growing conditions, and discusses factors such as soil, shelter and the characteristics that can make individual trees more or less suitable for a site. It describes the types of tree you can buy – container-grown or bare-root, for example – and how to plant and take care of them. We finish off with a look at pests and diseases and an overview of the art of pruning.

This apple is growing in a small planting pocket scraped out of the rocky coastal slump near Ventnor on the Isle of Wight. The soil is poor and free-draining, but with sufficient nourishment around the roots the tree is doing well, so far.

WHAT A TREE NEEDS

Very few of us can offer a tree perfect conditions, so it is usually a case of persuading it to work with an existing site, within reason. Fruit trees will not grow in a bog or standing water. They will not thrive on sand and they don't tend to be keen on soil that is highly acid or alkaline. But we can aim to choose a spot with a nice aspect and which isn't too dry or boggy, to give the tree a good chance of success in conditions that are somewhere between the extremes.

This tree is planted as a meadow specimen in a village garden. The soil is thin, light and highly alkaline, so the owner has carefully selected the variety and the rootstock to tilt the balance in her favour, and enriches the soil to help the tree thrive.

The biggest influences on what grows where are geography, climate, aspect and soil type. What grows in Britain varies from north to south and from south-east to south-west, but these climatic variations are nothing compared with what you will find in America or Australia. So the first thing to do is to look at what grows well in your area.

Climate

Each region has its distinct climate, but local variations in exposure or shelter and the existence of frost pockets or 'heat islands' can substantially influence how well fruit of any type will grow. In urban areas, the brick, stone or concrete of the buildings absorb the sun's heat and release it slowly back at night, raising average temperatures and reducing the risk of frost. Consequently, plants tend to come into leaf and flower earlier, and fruit will ripen sooner, than in cooler, more rural areas. On the flip side, this 'urban heat island' effect leads to a greater risk of drought and very high summer temperatures.

At the other end of the spectrum, cold conditions (and therefore higher altitude) can be a limiting factor. While citrus fruits, peaches and olives prefer warmth, apple trees in particular are pretty tolerant of winter chill – in fact they actively need it to initiate fruiting – so cold is unlikely to kill them. In cooler areas, however, the blossom will arrive later and is vulnerable to late frost. A late spring and an early autumn shortens the growing and ripening season, and although an intense, bright summer can ameliorate this to a certain degree, the effects are nonetheless significant.

Moisture levels are also important. The damper the climate, the more important a role drainage and air circulation will play in maintaining the health of a tree.

ABOVE: A peach tree can grow happily in a nice sheltered location.

RIGHT: Apples need a cold spell to fruit properly, usually quoted as around 1,000 hours a year below 7°C (45°F). This has limited their cultivation in tropical areas, but breeders are working on 'low chill' varieties, such as Anna and Dorsett Golden, for warm climates.

In the restored orchard at Bethlem Royal Hospital in London, the apples are enjoying a bit of winter chill.

In a north-facing front garden, a red crab apple thrives as a decorative design element.

Aspect, shelter and shade

Aspect is simply which way the site faces. A south- or west-facing site is ideal, as fruit trees like plenty of warmth and sun to help the fruit to ripen fully and encourage pollinators on to the flowers. On a north-facing or shaded site, there is a greater chance that the fruit will not set, either because chilly pollinators are less efficient or because the blossom gets frosted. (Note: If you're reading this in the southern hemisphere, read 'south-facing' for 'north-facing' and vice versa.)

Similarly, a sheltered site is more congenial than an exposed one. Protection can come from buildings, other trees, walls, hedges or even hills. Exposed sites may be buffeted by wind and lashed by rain, although it is less of a problem if the tree's role is mainly structural or ornamental rather than productive.

It makes sense to give your tree all the advantages you can. Choose the warmest and sunniest spot you can find; create a microclimate by training the tree against a wall. A balmy, reasonably free-draining site means that the area is likely not to hang wet, and this reduces the risk of fungal disease.

Some trees are more responsive to warmth than others, so consider what the best use for your prime (or sub-prime) site might be. It is far better to lavish a south-facing wall on a peach or pear than to squander its benefits on an apple that doesn't need it. If the wall or

This warm wall at Canons Ashby in Northamptonshire is ideal for ripening pears.

plot is north-facing, apples and sour cherries are a better option.

But trees are, by and large, survivors. One of my trees is the heritage Welsh apple variety Pen Caled, which is growing on a west-facing bank with fantastic long views. This means that it gets all the air circulation and sunshine it could possibly need. But it also means that there is nothing stopping the wind, which gets a clear run up the valley. Some years my tree crops prolifically; others not. And there have been years when it has produced fruit only on the more sheltered side, when a cold spring breeze has frosted the flowers directly before it, sparing those that are protected by the tree itself.

Soil

Soil can be highly variable and is subject to all sorts of influences, from rainfall to underlying geology. It can be light or heavy, acid or alkali, dry or wet, rich or poor – all of which will affect the plants that grow in it. In the gardens of new homes, challenges arise when builders dump rubble on the garden, then cover it up with imported soil, which may itself be poor quality (but that is a rant for another day).

Gardening books will tell you that the ideal soil for growing almost anything is a deep, moisture-retentive, fertile, free-draining loam (or similar). Most of us don't have this. But as long as your soil type is not too extreme, the best thing is to get on with planting your tree.

Improve the soil if necessary (see opposite), and see how it gets on. Your tree may well surprise you, but if after a couple of years it is not thriving, dig it up and try planting it somewhere else.

Assessing your soil

Here, observation and experiment are your friends. Dig a little hole and squidge a bit of soil between your fingers. Is it sticky like clay, sandy, or full of bits of composted plant material like a woodland floor? Does it crumble or hold together? Dig a bigger hole. How long before you hit subsoil (or rock, or water, or anything else that plants are not partial to)?

Look around. What is growing and how does it look? Are there lots of healthy rhododendrons, azaleas, skimmias or camellias? If there are, your soil is acidic. If there are none, the soil may be neutral or more alkaline. (If you discovered chalk when you dug your hole earlier, or if you are in an area noted for its chalk streams and your kettle is full of sediment, you may know this already.)

NON-OPTIMAL VARIETIES

There are certain varieties that are worth avoiding, either because they are hard to grow or for other reasons. For example:

✱ Cox's Orange Pippin, Granny Smith, Golden Delicious and Bramley are available in every shop.

✱ Cox's Orange Pippin is hard to grow.

✱ Granny Smith and Golden Delicious don't like the UK climate and will usually not ripen well.

✱ Bramley is too vigorous for a small garden. It is also triploid (see Chapter 6, page 170) (as are, for example, Ashmead's Kernel and Roxbury Russet, an old American variety), so it won't act as a pollinator for your other trees.

A Bramley is a handsome and vigorous apple.

So, again, it is worth doing some proper research, including into size and growth requirements, rather than just going for the comfortably familiar. (Remember too that size has a lot to do with the rootstock the tree is grafted on to. See Chapter 6, pages 165-7.)

You can get the soil tested of course, but an inexpensive pH testing kit and a good look at how soil behaves and what is growing in it will tell you a lot, very quickly and very cheaply.

So what does this actually mean? Well, fruit trees in general like a moisture-retentive fertile soil with a pH of 6.5-7, i.e. slightly acid to neutral. Acidic soils can be moderated with the addition of lime, but it is harder to reduce the pH of alkaline soils, so in this case enrichment with organic matter is likely to be a better idea than backyard chemistry.

Nor do fruit trees like wet feet. Clay soils tend to retain nutrients and water well, but they take a long time to warm up in spring and can become waterlogged. Sandy or rocky soils can suffer from over-sharp drainage, and, as nutrients are leached out by the rain, they are often poor. Chalk soils are alkaline and they may be thin, with low fertility.

So pick the best site you have, with good drainage and shelter, and manage and enrich the soil with compost or other organic matter, which will help with nutrient levels and water retention, and in moderating the pH.

Non-optimal situations

I grow most of my trees in an area of Wales known as the 'Celtic Rainforest' – which, while it sounds romantic, is about as far from the congenial orchards of Kent's equally romantic 'Garden of England' as it is possible to get in the British climate. While some trees do absolutely fine, others can't take the high moisture levels and limp on with a forlorn and cankered prospect.

Buttercups and lush grasses thrive in the moist climate of the Celtic Rainforest, doing very much better than some of the fruit.

But most sites have attributes that are less than ideal. So, rather than blithely picking a variety of fruit tree that sounds familiar, or because you like its picture, do a bit of research. Look at the fruit books or websites in the Resources section of this book or ask a specialist fruit nursery for recommendations. Opting for plants that are known to be tolerant of your climate improves your chances of success enormously.

In the Celtic Rainforest I grow the Victorian apple variety Egremont Russet. Well, I say 'grow', but it would be more accurate to say

If you want just one pear, Conference is hard to beat.

BUYING TIPS

❋ In all cases, reject trees that show any sign of pests, disease or significant damage.

❋ Don't buy bare-root trees that have clearly been left hanging around out of the ground, getting desiccated. If the roots seem suspiciously dry and crispy, think twice.

❋ Trees establish best in warmer soil, so don't try to plant them in very cold weather, especially if the ground is frozen.

that it continues to exist. It absolutely hates its home, despite the fact that the RHS describes this variety as "suitable for northerly, colder, higher-rainfall areas". To its credit, it does produce a few apples now and again, yet it persists in a fairly miserable state. Next to it, Rosemary Russet, about which no such claims are made, is a picture of health. Sometimes you just have to experiment.

BUYING A TREE

Trees come in various different forms. They can be delivered bare-root or bought in pots, and sometimes come with the rootball wrapped in hessian.

Bare-root trees

These are field-grown trees that are dug up for sale when they enter winter dormancy. Cool weather and the absence of foliage means that exposing the roots for a short period does no harm. Bare-root trees are cheaper than container-grown specimens and are a good choice if you are buying standards or half standards (see Chapter 6, page 168), or if you plan to train the tree. There also tends to be a good range available, both of varieties and of rootstocks.

The tree should be freshly lifted (dug up) by the nursery, with slightly moist roots, and firm, faintly shiny bark. Plant as soon as possible after delivery. If conditions are not right (for example, the ground is frozen), keep the plants cool and the roots moist and frost-free. You can either surround the roots with damp compost in a bucket, heel the tree into a shallow trench at an angle (backfilling around the roots with soil or compost), or pot it up temporarily.

Container-grown trees

These are sold all year round. The tree should look healthy and be a well-balanced and symmetrical shape. Check the roots for signs of overwatering and congestion, and the leaves for signs of drought. Generally, the soil at the top of the pot should be clear rather than covered in moss.

Potted trees do not need to be planted out immediately, but don't leave them in the pot for too long, as they will start to run out of nutrients and may get dry or root-bound.

Trees grown in containers can be planted all year round. If they are in leaf, make sure they get plenty of water.

CARING FOR TREES IN PERMANENT CONTAINERS

Like all containerized plants, potted trees need a bit of extra care. They must be watered every day in dry summer weather and protected from freezing solid in winter, either by moving to a sheltered place or under cover, or by wrapping in fleece. They need unimpeded drainage: lifting them a little off the ground on pot feet may help, but at any rate don't leave them standing in a puddle.

They also need regular feeding during the growing season – a high-potash fertilizer should be used between flowering and harvest to promote fruiting – and it is best to re-pot them every spring, before the leaf buds burst. Make sure the pot is big enough for the tree's needs, but not so big that the rootball is loose and can move with the rest of the tree in windy conditions.

HOW TO PLANT A TREE

There are different schools of thought about the best way to plant trees and about the need for staking, soil enrichment, and so on. The aim, in all cases, is to have a tree that is firmly anchored in the ground so it does not blow over, and sufficiently well nourished to establish strongly. Here, root health is of paramount importance, so it is helpful to reduce competition from grass and weeds, to make sure the tree doesn't get waterlogged or droughted, and to encourage the roots to grow out of the original planting hole into the surrounding soil (see opposite).

✳ The tree should be planted to the depth that it was growing before. Dig a hole that is deep enough to accommodate roots and the base of the trunk up to this point (a faint soil mark on the trunk should be visible), but not too deep. It must be wide enough for the roots to spread out properly.

TREES IN A LARGE ORCHARD

The classic, old-fashioned country use of fruit trees is as part of a large orchard. In most modern lives, this is likely to be possible only as a community orchard, garden project or as part of an institution, rather than in a domestic setting. Increasingly frequently, orchards are being added to school grounds, where they can be used in pursuit of a rounded education, and at hospitals, where they have been proven to contribute to well-being and healing (see box in Chapter 3, page 83).

In such situations, it is possible, even preferable, to plant standard trees, or the slightly more manageable half standards, to create a high canopy. The young trees should be protected from damage – whether from the grazing teeth of sheep or deer, from overzealous strimming or from adjacent football matches.

When establishing an orchard in a field, it is important to protect the trees. Animals (and unrestrained humans) can cause considerable damage.

Surround them with a wire cage and protect the trunk with a guard until they are well established and the bottom branches are at least 1.5m (5') from the ground.

* If you are using a stake, put it into the ground prior to planting the tree, so as not to damage the roots.

* Put the tree into the ground. Spread out the roots on bare-root trees; tease them out of the compost on containerized trees. Ensure that the graft union (identifiable as a bulge on the stem) is well above ground.

* If you are adding mycorrhizal fungi to support the plant, or otherwise feeding the tree or enriching the soil, do so now.

* Backfill the hole with soil and carefully firm it around the roots with your boot. Don't refill the hole with compost, as the idea is to get the tree growing away and reaching out into the surrounding soil. Too much rich organic matter creates a sump that can fill up with water or discourage the tree from growing outwards.

* Mulch the area around the tree with well-rotted manure, compost, animal straw, leafmould or other organic matter, ensuring that it does not touch the trunk. Water well.

* Apply rabbit guards or protect from grazing animals as necessary (see box opposite).

It is advisable to keep the surrounding soil clear of grass and weeds until the tree is established. Older trees too can benefit from reduced competition.

Aftercare

You can help your tree establish and grow strongly by looking after it. This is particularly important in its early years.

* Keep down competition with weed-suppressant matting or mulch, at least until the tree is established and growing strongly.

* Water the tree in dry periods.

* Keep the tree fed. Mulch around the tree annually with organic matter, or apply a proprietary slow-release fertilizer at the manufacturer's recommended rate.

* Generally speaking, dwarf trees will need to be staked permanently, but trees on vigorous rootstocks can have the stake removed once they are growing strongly (generally around 2-5 years).

PROBLEMS OF FRUIT TREES

Fruit trees are attacked by a range of pests and diseases, both general and specific. They can also develop nutritional problems and other issues due to site or conditions. This is not the book for an extensive discussion on fruit pests and diseases, although a few common ones are described here. But if your tree is not thriving or is clearly suffering damage, have a look at a good practical reference book such as *The Fruit Tree Handbook* by Ben Pike or the *RHS Garden Problem Solver*, or refer to the RHS website.

1. Brown rot often develops when a fruit has been damaged. 2. A grease band stops the wingless female of the winter moth climbing the tree to lay her eggs. 3. Woolly aphids suck sap from woody stems. 4. Scab (*Venturia inaequalis* in apples; *Venturia pirina* in pears) causes spotting of leaves and fruit that is spotted, cracked or blotched. 5. The cause of maggoty apples or pears is the codling moth. Often, the exit hole of the larva is visible. 6. Canker is caused by the fungus *Neonectria ditissima*, said to be more prevalent in wet areas and heavy soils.

PRUNING

Like any dark art, pruning can be decidedly daunting to a novice grower. And, to be fair, chopping bits off the very tree you are trying to grow does appear a bit perverse. But the value of this is in helping to keep the plant healthy, productive and in check, and it is the only way to create elegantly trained trees for small spaces.

Pruning will benefit young and productive trees. Starting formative pruning early means that you get a good shape, can influence where the branches are and, to some degree, can control the size. As the tree grows, pruning not only removes damaged and diseased wood but will also help reduce congestion, while stimulating new shoots.

Production of new growth, year on year, creates a continual supply of 2-year-old wood, which is where you will get the best fruit. Pruning also lets light and air into the centre of the tree, which helps with ripening and reduces the chances of fungal diseases such as scab and canker.

When it comes to older trees, much has been written about 'rejuvenating' them. But really it depends what you want to achieve. People who move into a house with old or neglected fruit trees in the garden often start lopping bits off willy-nilly because they feel they 'ought' to be pruned or controlled.

But one of the nice things about apple trees is that they get gnarly fairly fast and provide lots of lovely habitat for wildlife. A fairly young tree that has been allowed to become

Older trees should be treated gently, as they provide valuable habitat.

a tangled mess will benefit from pruning, but if it is very old there is a strong argument for not bothering to prune it at all. By this point it will have sorted itself out and will just crop modestly without intervention, providing food for bees and birds, a refuge for any number of beetles and moths, and acting as a host for mosses and lichens (more on wildlife habitat in Chapter 3).

So think twice before approaching an old fruit tree with regimented intent or rainforest-clearance mentality. They are often better

Pruning a tree to let the sunshine in means the fruit will ripen faster and sweeter.

treated kindly, like the venerable members of society that they are. Too harsh an approach will do them no good and may even kill them.

How to do it: pruning basics

The following is an illustration of some of the main techniques of pruning, the rationale behind it and the factors to take into consideration. For books and websites with more comprehensive advice, see Resources. Many community orchard groups, the RHS and some gardens offer courses and demonstrations.

When we talk about pruning, this usually refers to winter pruning. As already described, this opens up and refreshes the tree. The important thing to remember is that the more you cut off, the more vigorously the tree will grow back! Once a tree has got big, you can manage it but you can't very well make it smaller. You can't turn a 6m (20') tree into an attractive 3m (10') tree – it is better to plant the right size in the first place.

Winter pruning is appropriate for pome fruit – which includes apples, pears, quinces and medlars. Stone fruit – plums, gages, peaches, nectarines, cherries and apricots – need different treatment. They should not be pruned in winter as this can make them vulnerable to the fungal disease silver leaf, which is spread mainly in winter, as the spores are released under damp conditions. Instead, stone fruit should be pruned during the summer, up until early autumn.

This orchard of plums is kept open and airy by pruning in summer to avoid silver leaf disease.

Removing congested and crossing branches improves ventilation and also stimulates the production of fruiting wood.

Winter pruning of pome fruit

Once the fruit is picked and the leaves have fallen, remove any dead or diseased wood, and any branches that are rubbing or crossing, using sharp secateurs (pruners) or a pruning saw. If you are in doubt about whether a branch is dead or not, either snip a bit off and see if the wood is greenish and sappy on the inside, or leave it for this winter, then look at the tree when it's in leaf and tie a bit of string or ribbon around those branches that you will want to remove next winter.

Next, stand back and look at the shape of your tree. Open up the centre by thinning or removing branches that are facing inwards.

The idea for all productive trees is to create a nice branch system with varying ages of wood. In its first year a branch will grow and will produce only leaf buds, then in its second year it will produce both leaf buds and fruit buds. So part of the pruning regime is to create a constant supply of 2-year-old wood, as this will produce the most fruit, while older wood produces progressively less. Each year, some of the oldest wood can be removed, to be replaced by newer growth. This can also, to a certain extent, reduce a tendency towards biennial cropping (cropping in alternate years).

It is said that people fall into two camps when pruning. The first type will snip off a couple of twigs, decide that should do, and retire for a cup of tea. The other approaches the task like a botanical samurai, cartwheeling towards their victim in a blur of sharp implements.

But if you are new to it, feel your way. Arm yourself with the right tools. Have a good look at each tree before you start, and work out what needs to be done. And don't worry if you take off too little – you can always remove a bit more next year.

Summer pruning

Summer pruning is used to train fruit into cordons, fans, espaliers and other restricted forms, and to maintain those forms. Whereas winter pruning redirects the tree's energy and encourages the tree to 'go', summer pruning restricts growth and makes the tree 'stop'.

The exception to this rule is stone fruit, which should be formatively pruned during late spring or summer, and can be trained at the same time.

A trained pear awaiting pruning. It should be pruned in the middle of summer to allow light to reach the fruit.

Formally trained fruit always looks impressive, but the pruning of established trees is relatively simple. The idea is to cut off new shoots, allowing light to reach the fruit.

Summer-prune when the bottom third of the new shoots is stiff and woody, which is in late summer for apples and around a month earlier for pears, although to reduce regrowth this too can be left until late summer. This needs to be done every year, cutting off fruiting tips to between two and four buds from the base of the shoot.

New shoots that are more than 20cm (8") long, and are growing from the main stem (lateral shoots), should be cut back to three leaves above the basal cluster of leaves (the tight group of leaves at the base of this year's growth). Do not prune new shoots that are shorter than this, as they usually terminate in fruit buds. Shoots arising from the laterals (sublateral shoots) should be reduced to one bud above the basal cluster. Then remove any upright, vigorous growth completely. Remove any secondary growth in early autumn.

CHAPTER EIGHT

ENJOYING THE HARVEST

This chapter falls into two broad sections: how and when to pick your fruit, and what to do with it. Judging what point is best for harvest – and what you can get away with – can make the difference between success and failure; between sneaking a pleasurable meal from an unprepossessing source or wondering if you have let a free lunch go to waste.

Fruit varies. Cherries are best picked at the peak of ripeness, and enjoyed or preserved immediately. Pears are generally better plucked before they are fully ripe – kept safe from pecking beaks – then consumed at perfection, and not a moment later. Damsons and sloes tend to benefit from a late harvest, but apples can be picked and eaten fresh from late summer until late autumn. Different varieties, meanwhile, exhibit substantial differences in how well they store. The best thing to do is to become familiar with your trees: keep visiting them and testing the fruit. Soon you will get to know their internal clock.

The first harvest of the season is a moment worth waiting for. Check the developing fruits regularly and protect from birds if necessary (with cherries in particular, it probably will be necessary) to make sure there is some left for you when the time arrives.

HOW DO YOU KNOW THE FRUIT IS RIPE?

The main season for pome fruit (which is apples, pears, quinces, medlars and certain other members of the rose family, like hawthorn) runs from late summer to early winter, so gardens or orchards often have several types of tree to span the season. Timing is influenced by weather and temperature, and fruit will ripen faster in sun than shade, but when a fruit peaks is predominantly down to its variety.

The first indication of ripeness is increased attention from birds and the appearance of a few windfalls under the tree (unless it is in a grazed field, in which case the animals take to waiting underneath, hoovering up the evidence, while you wonder why the fruit seems to be so late this year).

The fruit mellows into its final colour, from greenish to warmer tones of yellow, orange or red, or richer hues of purple, particularly where it catches the sun. This does not yet mean perfection, but it is a good time to start checking. Cup it in your hand and give it a gentle twist. Ripe fruit will come away from the tree easily; if it puts up any significant resistance, it's not ready yet. With stone fruit, select a likely candidate and gently squeeze. If it yields a little, it is getting there, but if it's as hard as a bullet, try again in a few days.

If in doubt, taste it. While some fruit may be naturally acid-sharp, ripeness brings notes of

Forbidden or otherwise, a sun-warmed peach is a tempting snack.

When the pips are black, the fruit is ripe.

sweetness and a mellowness of flavour that is absent earlier.

Finally, the seeds of apples and pears turn brown as they ripen. This happens fairly late on, but if you cut one open and the seeds are green or white, it isn't ready. If the seeds are brown or black, the fruit can be picked with confidence.

WHEN AND HOW TO PICK

Not all the fruit on a tree ripens at once – the top of the tree and the sunny side will be ready to harvest first – which means that it can be picked twice, if not three times. If you leave the earliest-ripening fruit until the ones at the bottom and in the shade are ready,

you'll lose them to birds or they'll drop off and bruise. So pick them when they are ready, then leave it a week before returning.

With stone fruit there is a perfect point between 'hard enough to bounce off the floor' and 'melts into mush in the bag' – the fruit must be ripe, but firm enough to survive handling. The alternative is an unintended purée situation.

Some fruit is better picked before it is fully ripe, and allowed to mature off the tree. It will also store better and is less subject to damage in transit. Pears are the classic example: although initially hard as a rock, in the fruit bowl or on a warm windowsill they will very soon mellow. This treatment can also help to rescue a meagre plum harvest.

This crab apple in my north-facing front garden catches the evening sun on its left-hand side, where the fruit is noticeably riper than on the more shaded right.

Safely stored on the kitchen windowsill, pears can be eaten as they ripen.

HARVESTING ANOMALIES

To optimize palatability, some fruit should be dealt with in certain ways:

❋ **Medlars**, once picked, should be left until they are 'bletted' – soft and squidgy – before consuming.

❋ **Sloes** should, ideally, be picked after the first frost softens the skins. If frost comes late, pick them when they are ripe and put them in the freezer overnight.

Medlars are traditionally eaten either mashed up with sugar and cream, used as pie filling or simply baked and eaten with a spoon..

How to pick a tree

Certain items will make the job of harvesting more efficient. The following are essential:

❋ A bag to pick the fruit into. (You can get specialist soft bags designed for the job, but a carrier bag will do.)

❋ A trug or other container into which to empty the bag.

❋ Boxes. You can store apples and other fruit in any cardboard, wooden or plastic mesh box that will allow the fruit to breathe.

Other things are optional but useful:

❋ A ladder is handy if your tree is tall and tangled. An ordinary ladder is fine, or you can buy specially designed fruit-pickers' ladders.

❋ A long-handled picker. Basically a basket or bag at the end of a long stick, this works best when the fruit is reasonably sized and well spaced, otherwise in capturing one lofty fruit you will knock another two off. Practice, a steady hand and a strong bicep all help.

❋ Children. If you have large and scruffy trees, it is hard to beat giving a child a bag and sending him or her aloft. This creates an exciting sense of freedom and purpose. And it is actually quite hard to fall out of an over-grown apple tree.

Note: Of course safety precautions should always be observed. This is especially relevant in community and commercial orchards, in which, in the UK, the Work at Height Regulations 2005 will apply.

Apple-picking at Waterperry Gardens.

Safely gathered in.

A long-handled picker captures lofty or reluctant fruit.

Apple-picking is a timeless activity.

ABOVE: Perforated plastic trays or slatted wooden boxes allow good air movement around the fruit.

LEFT: The birds will let you know when your apples are ripening by eating the best ones first!

Grading, packing and moving

Once the fruit is at ground level, you will need to grade it and pack it into boxes, for transport to wherever it will live while waiting to be consumed.

First remove all fruit that is damaged or deteriorating. Anything that is pecked, bruised or wormy will not last long and needs to be used up as fast as possible.

The good-quality fruit should be packed into breathable boxes that are strong enough for the job. Banana boxes from supermarkets are good (although they can get pretty heavy when full), or you can make or buy smart wooden storage trays. The shallow mushroom boxes that are sometimes thrown out by pubs and restaurants are useful – with several layers of fruit in each, they stack well and they are a good size for carrying. Take care not to pack fruit so high or densely that the lower ones are crushed.

Pack and stack storage containers in such a way that there is movement of air between and within them. This reduces the build-up both of condensation and of ethylene gas, which is emitted by ripe fruit and serves to ripen it further.

It is hard to beat purpose-designed apple storage.

Devonshire Quarrenden is beautiful but ephemeral.

By late summer, one can be seriously tired of monochrome cold-store apples, and the arrival of the new season's fruit is often met with the same enthusiasm as the arrival of Father Christmas.

STORING

By late summer, one can become seriously tired of monochrome cold-store apples, and the arrival of the new season's fruit is often met with the same enthusiasm as the arrival of Father Christmas. That first bite of barely ripe, acid-fresh, just-off-the-tree apple – it is a memory that lingers.

Which is just as well, as the earlier an apple tree fruits, the less well that fruit will keep. Even the prettiest of my early eating apples, Devonshire Quarrenden, will repay the most careful attempts at storage by pitting, developing invisible bruises, and very rapidly melting into an unappetizing mush. Early fruit simply won't last long – maybe a week; a fortnight at best – in normal, room-temperature storage. So, revel in this first juicy flush, enjoy

One bad apple, pear, peach or plum does indeed spoil the whole barrel. So check all stored fruit regularly. If any are deteriorating, remove them to stop the rot.

Quince can be converted into delicacies such as quince jelly or membrillo.

them or give them away, but don't attempt to keep them.

A few weeks later, other varieties will better reward a conservative attitude. Generally speaking, mid-season apples will last 1 to 2 months, while late apples will usually store well, in some cases into early spring. Pears, too, can last from a couple of weeks to several months, depending partly on how well they are kept. (When in doubt, put them in the bottom of the fridge!) Some fruit will actually benefit from picking and standing, developing a richer, sweeter, more mellow flavour.

Due to differences in ripening rates, different varieties are best kept separate. Pears and stone fruit can ripen particularly quickly and rapidly go past their best. Check them daily and watch out for a slight change in colour or tell-tale softening.

Quinces last for about 4 weeks before they start to deteriorate. Their strong scent may taint other food, but they are handsome fruit. So if the aroma appeals, try keeping them as a table centre; a fragrant ornament – rather in the way that a pineapple was historically displayed as a status symbol.

VARIETIES FOR EATING AND PRESERVING

Apples
Eaters: Discovery, Katy, Devonshire Quarrenden, Greensleeves, Beauty of Bath, Scrumptious.
Cookers: Grenadier, Reverend W. Wilks, Scotch Dumpling.

Pears
Beth and Onward – eat quickly! Williams' Bon Chrétien keeps quite well in the fridge, while Merton Pride will last for a few weeks.

VARIETIES FOR STORING AND BAKING

Apples
Eaters: Granny Smith, Jonagold, Winston, Pixie, American Mother, Blenheim Orange, Saturn.
Cookers: Bramley's Seedling, Lane's Prince Albert, Howgate Wonder, Edward VII.

Pears
Concorde, Conference, Invincible, Catillac (a stewing/baking pear) and Doyenné du Comice will store well if picked when underripe.

Where to store your fruit

Pick a spot that is cool, dark, well ventilated, frost-free and mouse-free. Sheds, garages and cellars are ideal for stacking crates of fruit, while smaller quantities can be kept in the fridge as you would salad, either loose or in plastic bags pierced with holes to stop the fruit sweating. The RHS recommends a temperature of 2.7-7°C (37-45°F) for apples and even cooler for pears, if possible.

It is important that temperature and humidity are reasonably consistent. Freezing and thawing will spoil the fruit, and if kept too dry it will gradually desiccate. It is also important to keep stored fruit away from strong smells such as paint, white spirit, onions or anything else that might transfer its flavour in an undesirable fashion.

Reverend W. Wilks is a very soft early apple.

With care, Bramleys will store until early spring.

Home-made juice: Golden Reverend W. Wilks, Devonshire Quarrenden with a noticeably pink tone, and apple and blackberry juice just for fun.

Know your fruit

Irrespective of which trees you have planted or discovered, or what strange and mysterious treasures you glean from hedgerows, you will get the most from your fruit if you get to know them.

The pale green, early cooking apple Reverend W. Wilks is incredibly soft. It bruises as soon as you look at it and only keeps for 5 minutes, but it cooks to a tasty, smooth purée which is lovely with brown sugar and cream, with blackberries or raisins in crumble or as a fresh apple sauce. The later-fruiting Lord Derby also cooks to a mush – or textured purée if you prefer – and, despite Bramley's absolute retail dominance, not all cooking apples are, or behave like, Bramleys.

It is early spring as I write this and, in a box in the kitchen downstairs, there are half a dozen apples that came off the tree in my garden. I have no idea what the tree is – it was present and mature when I arrived – but it is an absolute corker. It crops prolifically, producing large, handsome, tasty fruit. These cook well, keep their shape and make a sherbet-sharp juice when pressed. It is not particularly late to crop – mid-season, perhaps – but the fruit are still going strong. Although they no longer boast the sappy freshness of autumn, the flavour has intensified and a rich, sweet, almost quince-like aroma has developed.

Every tree has its own distinctive character. Bountiful is a generous, regular-cropping apple. Golden Noble and Pitmaston Pineapple

CARGO FROM AUSTRALIA

In the days before cold stores and mass production, looks were less crucial. What counted was flavour and keeping quality.

The Sturmer Pippin is ordinary-looking and sharp to taste, but it matures and sweetens in store, reaching its peak the following spring. Popular in Victorian times, it was taken to Australia and New Zealand by settlers as the perfect apple for exporting. It could be picked in the Antipodean autumn, loaded on to a ship and sailed to Europe. When they docked, it was summer locally and the apples would be ready for consumption, neatly filling the gap before the British crops appeared.

In 1868, the Granny Smith was discovered by Maria Ann Smith in Eastwood, New South Wales. Maria Smith died in 1870, but her apple was cultivated by a neighbouring grower, Edward Gallard. It was soon discovered that Granny Smith had an excellent shelf life, of up to 8 months, and it could be shipped without deteriorating. By 1975, it represented 40 per cent of Australia's apple crop and was grown intensively across the southern hemisphere, as well as in France and the USA.

are both yellow, but the juice of one has the clarity of old mead and the other the opacity of coconut cream. Familiarity reaps rewards.

PRESERVING

Preserving is the process of converting food into a state that resists deterioration, by inhibiting the actions of bacteria and fungi. Different forms of preservation act in different ways, either by killing microorganisms outright or rendering them unable to reproduce by physical damage, or by creating an environment that is too hostile for them to thrive.

❋ **Freezing** This doesn't kill bacteria or fungi, but it prevents the food spoiling because the temperature is so low that life processes and reproduction are all-but-halted. The food remains fresh until it is thawed, when microbiological life resumes normal speed.

❋ **Drying** This reduces water levels and concentrates sugars, making it hard for microorganisms to breed.

❋ **Boiling** Raising the temperature high enough kills microorganisms outright, as in boiling fruit for jam or cordial, or blanching vegetables.

❋ **Pasteurizing** This involves heating the product, without boiling it, for long enough that spoilage organisms are killed or can no longer reproduce.

❋ **Adding sugar or salt** Adding sugar or salt to a mixture (such as jam or salt pickles) raises

Bottled fruit is an easy luxury.

its osmotic potential, so water moves out of living cells into the surrounding environment. This means that should any spoilage bacteria survive the boiling process or arrive at a later date, they will desiccate and die.

❋ **Pickling** Pickling in vinegar increases the acidity to the point where microorganisms cannot operate.

❋ **Alcohol** This acts as a preservative, killing the spoilage organisms or making it hard for them to reproduce, depending on the percentage volume.

Surplus fruit can be preserved in many ways, from freezing and juicing to the preparation of a whole range of jams, jellies, curds, fruit butters and cheeses or savoury chutneys and pickles. The key ideas are introduced briefly in the following pages, and some good recipe books can be found in the Resources section.

Freezing

The simplest way to preserve fruit of all types is to freeze it, either cooked or uncooked.

❋ **Cherries, plums and other small fruit** can be frozen in a tray in the top of the freezer, then poured into a box or bag. Or, if structural integrity is not an issue, just pour the fruit straight into the bag.

❋ **Apples, pears, quinces and other large fruit** can be cored, chopped and frozen raw. To pack more fruit in, poach or stew it first, then freeze it in blocks in ice-cream tubs or similar containers.

Drying

Using an oven or dehydrator, surplus water is removed without cooking the fruit, which is then stored in a sealed jar. If using an oven:

❋ Wash the fruit and remove the core or stone. Cut into thin slices, or halve smaller stone fruit.

❋ Dip apple and pear slices in lemon juice first to stop them from going brown.

❋ Place in a single layer on a baking tray covered with a layer of parchment.

❋ Put in a cool oven at 50°C (120°F). Or, if you have one, the bottom of an Aga is ideal. Leave for several hours until chewy, rather than crunchy or squishy.

In warm, dry climates apple rings can be hung in an airy place to desiccate. In Europe, it is usual to build drying ovens. An alternative is a vacuum desiccator.

Tart, raw damsons are divine made into jam or 'cheese'.

STROOP: CONCENTRATED FRUIT POWER

Stroop is a sugar-free jam-pulp of apples and, particularly, pears. It is a traditional way of using up surplus harvest in Belgium, and there are variations in other European countries.

Preserving with sugar

Jam and chutney are a very good way of preserving less-than-perfect fruit or dealing with gluts. I also use chutney as a solution to a surfeit of early apples that won't keep for long, or early fallers that are too sharp for ordinary cooking. Meanwhile, bottling fruit such as plums and peaches keeps them whole and juicy for later use. A couple of contrasting pots makes a pretty Christmas present.

Jam, jelly and cordial

It is very satisfying to have a shelf full of jams, jellies and dilutable fruit concentrates, and the basic principle of all these preserves is the same: take a quantity of fruit, boil it with sugar and seal in a sterilized container. The differences lie in whether you want a clear liquid cordial, a clear set jelly, or an opaque, lumpy but marvellously tasty jam.

While in principle the process is very easy, there are subtleties involved. Some fruits contain more pectin than others, so will set better. The clarity of jellies and cordials depends on letting them drip through a muslin or jelly bag – a process that can't be rushed.

Bottling

This preserves the fruit at peak perfection. You basically heat up the fruit in a syrup, transfer it to the glass preserving jar, then boil in the jar for the required period before sealing. *Voilà!* Attractive, tasty fruit that will last about a year on the shelf.

Chutney

When making chutney, I tend to busk around a basic recipe according to what I have. As long as you maintain the fundamental proportions of ingredients and taste it occasionally, you can't go too far wrong.

NAOMI'S CHRISTMAS CHUTNEY

1kg (2lb) apples
500g (1lb) onions
140g (5oz) dried, pitted dates
140g (5oz) dried, pitted apricots
340g (12oz) soft brown sugar
250ml (½ pint / ³⁄₅ US pint) vinegar
1tsp pickling spice
1tsp whole cloves
140g (5oz) raisins
Juice and zest of 1 orange and 1 lemon
1tsp cinnamon
1tsp salt
Ground black pepper to taste

Note: The quantities refer to prepared fruit and veg.

Method

Roughly peel the apples, then core and chop.

Peel and dice the onions.

Roughly chop the dates and apricots.

Put the prepared fruit and veg in a preserving pan or large saucepan and add the sugar and vinegar.

Tie the pickling spice and cloves into a small square of muslin, give it a good wallop with a rolling pin, and drop the package into the mix.

Add the raisins, orange and lemon juice, cinnamon and a little seasoning.

Bring the mixture to the boil and cook on a brisk heat, stirring regularly to stop it burning. Do not cover with a lid, as the chutney needs to reduce.

Add the orange and lemon zest about halfway through cooking.

Taste the chutney towards the end of cooking and add any further salt and pepper that may be necessary.

When you can pull a wooden spoon across the bottom of the pan and it leaves a clear path for a moment, the chutney is ready.

Ladle into clean, warmed jars and stir gently with a spoon handle to remove air pockets. The less air in the jar, the better the preserve will keep. Using a tea towel to protect your hands, put the lids on while the contents are still piping hot. When it cools it will form an airtight seal.

When they are properly cold, wipe and label the jars, including the date. The chutney will keep for several years.

Note: Chutneys should not be kept in metallic containers or exposed to metal lids on jars, as the vinegar can react with the metal and taint the food.

Apples are a good base for chutney, but you can partially substitute other fruit, such as pears or plums, or use green tomatoes or vegetables. Recipes can be scaled up or down depending on how much fruit is at your disposal, but it is important not to reduce the proportion of sugar or vinegar, as this is what preserves the fruit.

There are recipes galore and plenty of books on preserves, but opposite is a recipe of my own invention to be going on with, adding interest with seasonal flavours.

Juicing

I got into juicing as a solution to a monumental glut. Profligate planting meant that the house was stacked with wobbling, precarious mountains of apples and the family faced impossible volumes of crumble and chutney. But on a work trip to the orchards and juice press at Waterperry Gardens in Oxfordshire, I had a flash of inspiration. Juice would deal with the immediate surplus and, if pasteurized, would also keep well for over a year.

We started cautiously, at first sending the apples to be pressed by a local contractor. But as our experiment escalated into a micro-enterprise, we invested in the kit and began to do it ourselves, pressing single varieties or simple blends into a range of well-balanced and subtly different juices.

Juicing: need to know

The first thing you need is a decent quantity of apples (or apples and pears). On a small scale you can include fresh windfalls that

A big juicing enterprise can pasteurize hundreds of bottles at a time.

won't otherwise keep, since blemishes have no impact on the taste. Foragers and novice or time-poor gardeners take heart – as long as it's ripe, even small and spotty fruit can make the grade.

However, avoid rotten fruit at all costs. The human palate is very sensitive to 'off' flavours, and the juice will taste musty and won't keep well. There is also a mycotoxin called patulin which is produced by certain fungi that develop on fruit, although one would have to drink large volumes of contaminated juice for it to be an issue. Deploying normal levels of vigilance and common sense, and not including elderly apples in your juice, should be sufficient precaution.

How you collect your fruit may depend on the scale at which you are operating. If you have lots of apples and plan to use a contractor, ask about any restrictions: some insist that the fruit has not been near the ground (in which

If you have a decent quantity of apples, think about making juice.

case you will have to pick the fruit carefully by hand when it is ripe). If you are just pressing a few bottles' worth at home, you can wash any windfalls to remove mud or detritus.

Sharper apples make better juice than very sweet ones. If necessary, mix varieties in order to balance sweetness and acidity – it is worth experimenting.

Juicing at home

Making juice using a domestic juicer or masticating juicer is simple: you feed apples and other fruit in the top according to the instructions, and juice comes out the bottom.

At first the liquid will be cloudy and greenish-yellow in colour, but it will very quickly go brown, so add a little vitamin C (ascorbic acid) in the form of lemon juice to keep the colour (just like adding citrus juice to fruit salad to stop the apples going brown). You can achieve greater clarity by letting the liquid settle and pouring the juice off the sediment, but take care not to over-strain it, as the suspended fruit particles add body and flavour.

Fresh-pressed juice will not keep for very long, so it should be refrigerated and consumed within a couple of days. Freeze it or turn it into ice lollies for more extended storage.

Going pro

If you have a substantial quantity of fruit, it is worth getting it contract-pressed and pasteurized in the bottle. This significantly extends the juice's shelf life without taking up valuable

Making poire William at Château de Valmer. Slip a wide-necked bottle over the top of a developing pear and secure in place. When the pear is ripe, add sweetened vodka, or the spirit of your choice, *et voilà!*

freezer space. You usually need a minimum quantity of fruit, and the process can be relatively expensive, although it is still cheaper than buying bottles of good-quality locally produced fruit juice elsewhere.

The alternative, if you have a serious number of trees, is to invest in your own equipment. Presses are available in various sizes, from hobbyist to small- or large-scale commercial, so you can pick something that suits your operation. This is also a good solution for community groups, allotment societies and other types of collective that can benefit from a shared resource. (Note: In a communal set-up

SELLING YOUR JUICE

Once you have got your bottles of fabulous, tasty juice, you might want to share it or sell it to make a profit, cover costs or raise funds. This is the perfect way to capture the taste of a region or celebrate the work of a community, but there are a few rules to observe. Foodstuffs need to be fit for consumption and traceable. Fruit juice is a low-risk product, but everyone wants to know that their food is wholesome and safe, and this is also a legal requirement.

So, in order to sell your juice (rather than give it away), you will need to produce it in an acceptably hygienic environment and follow some straightforward, common-sense procedures to ensure that it is fit for consumption. You must also label it with the product contents, its volume, a 'best before' date and a postal address – this is in addition to any logo or design you may create. Refer to local regulations for specific requirements.

Your local environmental health and trading standards representatives will be able to advise you. This may sound a bit serious, but their job is to check that the right boxes are ticked and that your product is safe. So don't worry about ringing them up for guidance, and it is best to do this early in proceedings. Consider it a form of business support rather than as red-tape types making life difficult.

In the unlikely event that you have a surplus of peaches or nectarines, you can add them to Rumtopf.

I suggest you draw up a firm set of rules about cleaning the equipment after use!)

Whatever the scale, the principles are the same. You take clean, whole apples and put them in a macerator. The resulting pulp is then pressed, using the barrel or 'cheese' apple-press system. A little bit of commercial ascorbic acid is added to the juice, and it is poured into bottles which are then pasteurized in what is effectively a closed pan with a thermostat. See Resources for suppliers of pressing equipment.

Cider

With a surplus of apple or pear juice, home-made cider may seem the next logical step. In principle it is straightforward. Fill a sterilized demijohn with juice, inoculate it with a cider yeast (or let the wild yeasts do their thing), fit a bubble trap to the top and put it somewhere warm until the fermentation stops. Pour it off the sediment and consume in moderation.

Cider-making is an ancient pastime, with apple varieties specifically developed for the purpose. Typically very juicy, they are often selected for characteristics that make them less palatable as a culinary or dessert fruit, including colour, bitterness or sharpness. And they often have some great names: Foxwhelp, Black Dabinett, Dunkerton Late Sweet and Slack ma Girdle, for example.

There are many arcane nuances in the making of craft cider, and it varies from country to country – the traditions of France differ from those of Britain, for example, and plain old European cider goes by the much more serious-sounding name of 'hard cider' in America. To find out more, check out the websites in Resources, invest in a good book or join a local group.

Edible apple blossom can be used to decorate cakes.

Fruit in alcohol

Sloe gin is a hedgerow beverage of almost mythological status, but all sorts of fruit can be used to flavour all sorts of alcohol. Damson vodka, cherry brandy, mulberry vodka, pears in grappa . . . there are many variations.

In all cases the principle is the same. Select some ripe fruit and put it in a bottle, top it up with the spirit of your choice and add a few spoonfuls of sugar. Seal it and put it in a cool dark place for at least 6 weeks, just shaking it occasionally.

The proportion of sugar to fruit depends on how much fruit you have available, how sharp it is and your personal taste. The fruit should

RUMTOPF

This is a traditional German dish where fruit is preserved with rum and sugar. You start in summer with fruit like strawberries and cherries, then, as plums, nectarines, peaches and pears ripen, you add them too.

Take a large, sealable container – or a traditional Rumtopf jar (try eBay). Remove any stones from the fruit and halve or slice them, depending on size. For each 500g (1lb) fruit, add 250g (8oz) sugar and cover with strong dark rum (overproof rum is usually used). As further fruits ripen, repeat the process until the jar is full. Allow to stand and steep. It should be ready by Christmas and is ideal as a topping for pancakes or ice cream, with mascarpone as a cake filling, or in a glass topped up with prosecco as a lethal fruity cocktail.

be ripe but not disintegrating and, if using sloes, they should be softened by frost. If in doubt, go easy on the sugar and test for sweetness once the fruit is well steeped – you can always top it up. When you are ready to drink it, either strain off the fruit or leave it if you prefer – and enjoy.

"Now pause with your selfe, and view the end of all your labours in an Orchard: unspeakable pleasure, and infinite commodity."
WILLIAM LAWSON, *A NEW ORCHARD AND GARDEN* (1618)

RESOURCES

Each country has its own heritage, fruit community and literature to be explored. In this section I have created a selection of interesting leads, but this list is really just a starting point for your own journey. A more detailed version of this section is available as a pdf with live hyperlinks at www.greenbooks.co.uk/orchard-resources/

Organizations

There are many organizations which focus on orchards in various ways. Below are some useful examples.

Brogdale Farm / Brogdale Collection
Faversham, Kent, UK
www.nationalfruitcollection.org.uk;
www.brogdalecollections.org
Brogdale Farm is the home of the National Fruit Collection, which is curated and government funded, while Brogdale Collections is a charitable organization responsible for events, public access and school visits. You can buy propagating material from the Collection to graft yourself or to order.

European Specialist in Traditional Orchards (ESTO)
Weimar, Germany, and other European centres
www.esto-project.eu
Comprising 12 partner organizations in 6 European countries; focused on conservation and promotion of traditional orchards in Europe. The website has regional information and links to other organizations.

Orchard People
Online-only
www.orchardpeople.com
Toronto-based fruit-tree-care consulting and education organization. Offers both in-person and online workshops.

People's Trust for Endangered Species (PTES)
London, UK
https://ptes.org/orchards
https://ptes.org/orchard-network
https://ptes.org/orchard-biodiversity
https://ptes.org/fruitfinder
Wildlife conservation charity; welcomes input. Provides resources for finding varieties and surveying traditional orchards; has a good document about orchard management for wildlife:
https://ptes.org/orchard-management

Royal Horticultural Society (RHS)
London, UK
www.rhs.org.uk
The UK hub of practical gardening, with a very useful website. Offers a fruit identification service, for a fee, together with a members' pest-and-disease advice service. Has a number of flagship gardens, including RHS Garden Wisley, Surrey.

Thuringian Fruit-pruning School / Thüringer Obstbaumschnittschule
Weimar, Germany
www.obstbaumschnittschule.de
Pruning classes and habitat orchard.

United States Association of Cider Makers
Denver, CO, USA
www.ciderassociation.org
An organization of cider and perry makers. Information about production, regulations and growing.

The Urban Orchard Project
Online-only
www.theurbanorchardproject.org;
http://helpingbritainblossom.org.uk
Dedicated to planting, managing and restoring orchards in urban areas.

Nurseries and tree suppliers

There are many suppliers of fruit trees, but the following have particularly good ranges, sell unusual or trained specimens, or, in some cases, offer a bespoke grafting service.

Agroforestry Research Trust
Totnes, Devon, UK
www.agroforestry.co.uk
Trees, information and courses

on forest gardening and orchard management.

Albemarle Cider Works / Vintage Virginia Apples
North Garden, VA, USA
www.albemarleciderworks.com
Includes many heritage varieties. Also workshops and tastings, and Harvest Festival every year on the first Saturday in November.

Ashridge Trees
Castle Cary, Somerset, UK
www.ashridgetrees.co.uk
A good selection of fruit trees and helpful advice on the website.

Bernwode Fruit Trees
Ludgershall, Bucks, UK
www.bernwodefruittrees.co.uk
Grafts to order. Useful website, with descriptions of unusual fruit.

Eastman's Antique Apples
Wheeler, MI, USA
www.eastmansantiqueapples.com
Significant collection of American antique or heritage varieties.

Fedco Trees
Waterville, ME, USA
www.fedcoseeds.com/trees
Supports the Great Maine Apple Day in October (Common Ground Education Centre, Unity, ME).

Frank P Matthews Ltd / Trees for Life
Tenbury Wells, Worcs, UK
www.frankpmatthews.com
Large fruit tree supplier, with over 200 apple varieties and online stockist-search facility.

Fruit and Nut
Westport, Co. Mayo, Ireland
www.fruitandnut.ie
Specialist supplier of nut trees and an extensive range of fruit suitable for Irish growing conditions. Courses and workshops.

Future Forests
Bantry, Co. Cork, Ireland
www.futureforests.net
Wide range of fruit trees, including native and unusual varieties.

Grandpa's Orchard
Coloma, MI, USA
www.grandpasorchard.com
A good selection of fruit on a wide range of rootstocks.

Lubera
Online-only
www.lubera.co.uk
Swiss breeder and supplier of unusual and interesting soft fruit, fruit trees and other edibles. Specialists in small-space growing, including dwarf apples, pears, peaches and cherries.

Otter Farm Shop
Online-only
http://shop.otterfarm.co.uk
Nursery run by climate-change gardener Mark Diacono. Stocks conventional fruit and nuts plus interesting exotics. Trees are available as standards, dwarf bushes and in trained forms.

Reads Nursery
Bungay, Suffolk, UK
www.readsnursery.co.uk
Family nursery offering free expert advice on selection and planting.

Stark Bro's Nurseries and Orchards Company
Louisiana, MO, USA
www.starkbros.com
Famously established nursery and fruit supplier. The original home of the loved-or-loathed Red Delicious.

Trees of Antiquity
Paso Robles, CA, USA
www.treesofantiquity.com
Family nursery supplying organic fruit trees, centred on heirloom apple varieties.

Willis Orchard Company
Cartersville, GA, USA
www.willisorchards.com
A good range of trees and an enthusiasm for flavour.

Rent a tree

In some places you can rent a tree annually. You can often visit it in blossom time and the harvest is yours too. Here are a few examples.

Earth First Farms
Berrien Center, MI, USA
http://earthfirstfarms.com

Farm on the Hill
Prestwood, Staffs, UK
www.farmonthehill.co.uk/plant-your-own-fruit-tree-at-the-farm.html

Rent a Cherry Tree
Northiam, East Sussex, UK
www.rentacherrytree.co.uk

Tree-mendus Fruit
Eau Claire, MI, USA
www.treemendus-fruit.com

Equipment suppliers

Lots of equipment can be bought directly from the suppliers listed here, while some brands are widely retailed. The product descriptions given in the following listings serve to highlight the ranges.

Apple Picking Bags
Portland, OR, USA
www.applepickingbags.com
Serious stuff for orchards. Apple-picking bags, pruning kit and more.

Ball Mason
Kempsey, NSW, Australia
http://ballmason.com.au
Water baths, juicers, bottling and preserving jars and equipment.

Fiskars
Brand widely available
www3.fiskars.com
Long-handled fruit pickers; useful range of pruning tools.

Jarden Home Brands
Fishers, IN, USA
www.freshpreserving.com
Iconic Mason and Kerr jars. Also water baths, pressure canners, and techniques and recipes on website.

Le Parfait
Online-only
www.leparfait.fr;
www.leparfait.com
Famous for good-quality preserving jars and bottles. Techniques and recipes on website.

Niwaki
Dorset, UK
www.niwaki.com
Japanese pruning tools, lightweight ladders for fruit trees.

Suttons
Brand widely available; also online shop
www.suttons.co.uk
Slatted wooden trays for fruit storage, small-scale fruit presses.

Vigo Ltd
Dunkeswell, Devon, UK
www.vigopresses.co.uk;
www.vigoltd.com (for commercial-scale)
Pressing equipment for small- and large-scale operations; products for preserving, drying and bottling fruit. Picking ladders and pruning saws.

Weck
Online-only
www.weck.de
Great German website for steam juicers, water baths and preserving jars and bottles.

WOLF-Garten
German brand widely available; also online shop
www.wolf-garten.com
Long-handled fruit pickers, loppers, pruning tools.

Good websites and online resources

There is masses of information available online, but below is a core of useful resources.

**www.ciderguide.com;
www.ciderguide.com/cider-maps**
Hub of information about making and drinking cider, with an interactive map of cideries worldwide.

www.ciderworkshop.com
Online community for cider and perry enthusiasts internationally.

**www.fruitforum.net;
www.fruitforum.net/christmas-pippin-a-winner-.htm**
Online discussion group on all things fruity, managed by apple-and-pear guru Joan Morgan.

www.fruitid.com
Fruit identification.

**www.orangepippin.com;
www.orangepippintrees.eu;
www.orangepippintrees.co.uk**
Excellent websites covering identification and history of various fruit, but particularly good for apples.

www.pickyourown.org
Listings website for picking your own fruit, with useful crop calendars for timings. Wide-ranging remit includes UK, USA, Canada, South Africa, Australia and New Zealand.

www.realenglishfruit.co.uk/tree-size
Handy information about tree size and rootstocks.

Apple processing

Lots of people will process your apples for you. Here are just a few examples.

Milltop Orchard
Newton Abbot, Devon, UK
www.milltoporchard.co.uk
Offers contract-pressing, bottling and a cider-manufacturing service.

The Random Apple Company
Macclesfield, UK
www.swanscoe.co.uk
Offers a pressing service.

See also: **Waterperry Gardens** (page 215)

Community and foraging

Urban and community orchard organizations and foraging groups exist across the world, together with a range of local, regional and global online resources. Some of these are listed here.

The Boston Tree Party
www.bostontreeparty.org
A US urban agriculture coalition which aims to support civic fruit.

City Fruit
www.cityfruit.org
Seattle-based fruit cultivation to nourish the community and protect the climate.

FareShare
www.fareshare.org.uk
Food distribution network in the UK.

Fruit-full Schools
www.fruitfullschools.org
A British network of schools which takes positive action towards a sustainable future through orchard gardening.

North American Fruit Explorers (NAFEX)
www.nafex.org
Members-only network of fruit enthusiasts based in the USA and Canada, who devote themselves to the cultivation and appreciation of superior fruit and nut varieties.

Philadelphia Orchard Project
www.phillyorchards.org/about_pop
This American project plants and designs community orchards and gives the local people the skills to care for them, particularly in less-affluent neighbourhoods.

Portland Fruit Tree Project
www.portlandfruit.org
Encourages the community to share in the harvest and care of urban fruit trees, preventing waste, promoting knowledge, and creating sustainable local food sources in this corner of Oregon.

Sole Food Street Farms
http://solefoodfarms.com
Transforms vacant land in Canada into artisan street farms.

Out and about

There are many places where you can see orchards and orchard gardens – fruit collections big and small – inspiring, educational or simply cool. Those marked have an additional educational(*) or conservation(^) remit.

Australia

Huon Apple and Heritage Museum
Hobart, Tasmania
www.newnorfolk.org/~apple_museum
500 different apple varieties on display, and restored working machinery.

Denmark

Blomstergården^*
Viborg
www.blomstergaardenvedviborg.dk
A collection of hundreds of different old and new varieties of apple, pear, plum and cherry trees at a private research centre. Tours, education and fruit sales.

England

The Ironbridge Gorge Museum Trust
Telford, Shropshire
www.ironbridge.org.uk
National Collection of bullaces and damsons.

The National Trust
Swindon, Wiltshire
www.nationaltrust.org.uk
Many iconic gardens and orchards, good examples of which include Greys Court, Oxfordshire; Canons Ashby, Northamptonshire; and West Green House, Hampshire.

Queen Elizabeth Roof Garden, Southbank Centre
London
www.southbankcentre.co.uk/venues/Queen-Elizabeth-Hall-Roof-Garden
A Thames-side surprise packed with ultra-urban lashings of containerized fruit trees and wildflowers.

Waterperry Gardens^*
Wheatley, Oxfordshire
www.waterperrygardens.co.uk
Orchards and trained fruit, some in a design context, and a double avenue of cordons, some of which are over 70 years old. Teaching and Apple Days; contract-juice-pressing facility. The 2 hectares (5 acres) of orchards date back to the days of Beatrix Havergal, who ran her famous school of horticulture for ladies until 1972.

France

Normandy has a cider and calvados trail: see www.calvados-tourisme.co.uk/en/discover/tourist-trails/the-cider-route.php

Château de Talcy
Talcy, Loire Valley
www.chateau-talcy.fr
A fairly small château and garden, with many varieties of trained fruit and a conservatory orchard.

Château du Rivau^
Lémeré, Loire Valley
www.loire-castle-rivau.com
Charming young orchard of apples and medlars surrounded by roses; fruit in containers, modern potager and grapes trained into 'umbrellas'.

Le Potager du Roi
Versailles, near Paris
www.chateauversailles.fr
Magnificent garden filled with rare and forgotten varieties of apples and pears, trained using historic pruning techniques.

Villandry
Villandry, Loire Valley
www.chateauvillandry.fr
The mother and father of French formal fruit and veg gardening. Impressive.

Germany

The Julius Kühn-Institut (Institute for Breeding Research on Fruit Crops)
Dresden
www.jki.bund.de/en/startseite/institute/breeding-research-on-horticultural-and-fruit-crops.html
The location of the German apple collection.

Ireland

Ardgillan Castle
Dublin
http://ardgillancastle.ie
The walled garden contains fan-trained stone fruit and 30 old Irish varieties of apple.

Glenveagh Castle
Letterkenny
www.heritageireland.ie
A good selection of local Irish apples in the kitchen garden over-looking Lough Veagh.

Italy

Orto dei Frutti Dimenticati
Rimini
www.museoiluoghidellanima.it/orto-dei-frutti-dimenticati
'The Garden of Forgotten Fruits' is an orchard museum with 300 varieties of apple.

The Netherlands

Kasteel-Museum Sypesteyn
Loosdrecht
www.sypesteyn.nl
A formal seventeenth-century garden with a pear pergola surrounds the romantic castle, and across the moat stands an orchard of quince and walnut trees.

Menkemaborg
Uithuizen
www.menkemaborg.nl
Reconstructed from a plan of 1705, features a pear tunnel and many traditional apple varieties.

North America

Annapolis Valley Apple Blossom Festival
Nova Scotia, Canada
http://appleblossom.com
A week-long festival that has been celebrating the arrival of blossom since 1933, with activities of all sorts.

Boscobel
Garrison, NY, USA
www.boscobel.org
Trained fruit now surrounds the historic garden, and there are standard trees in the formal beds.

Franklin County CiderDays
Berkshire Mountains, MA, USA
www.ciderdays.org
Cider-making, tastings and work-shops to enjoy around the county.

Cornell University
The Plant Genetic Resources Unit of USDA-ARS, at Geneva, NY, USA
Collections of wild Central Asian apples and thousands of cultivated varieties. Open days usually in September, details published on: www.ars.usda.gov/News/News.htm
See also: National Clonal Germ-plasm Repository, Corvallis, OR; www.ars.usda.gov/main/site_main.htm?modecode=20-72-15-00

Jacksonport Cherry Festival
Jacksonport, WI, USA
www.jacksonporthistoricalsociety.org/cherry_fest.php
Cheerful cherry-themed event with lots of fresh cherries and cherry products, together with music and other activities.

Monticello
Charlottesville, VA, USA
www.monticello.org;
www.monticello.org/site/visit/events/apple-tasting
Between 1769 and 1814, Thomas Jefferson, author of the American Declaration of Independence, planted over 1,000 fruit trees in a 3-hectare (8-acre) fruitery, including cider apples in his North Orchard. Hosts a workshop described as "the oldest formal apple tasting in America".

Old Sturbridge Village
Old Sturbridge, MA, USA
www.osv.org
A living museum that recreates life in rural New England from the 1790s to the 1830s. Features orchards and an operating ox-driven nineteenth-century cider mill.

Poland

Warsaw Botanic Garden
www.staresady.republika.pl/intro_
en.htm;
www.ogrod-powsin.pl
*The Center for Biological Diversity
Conservation in Warsaw has a
historic apple cultivar collection.*

Scotland

The National Trust for Scotland
Edinburgh
www.nts.org.uk
*Restored and original orchards to
explore, including Culross Palace
in Dunfermline and Priorwood
Gardens in Melrose.*

Sweden

**Bergianska Botaniska
Trädgården**
Stockholm
www.bergianska.se
*Stockholm's Botanic Gardens,
featuring collections of Swedish
apples, fruits and berries.*

**Fredriksdal Museum and
Botanical Gardens**
Helsinborg
www.fredriksdal.se
*Open-air museum and orchard of
50 varieties of Swedish apples.*

Books

Many books touch upon apples
and other fruit, dabble in preserving or give a nod to foraging
and cultivation. The books listed
below, however, are each dedicated to their art and are a very
good place to start.

The Apple Book, Rosie Sanders
(Frances Lincoln, rev edn 2010)
Beautiful watercolours of apples,
with detailed descriptions to help
with identification. An inspiring
resource.

Apples of North America, Tom
Burford (Timber Press, 2013)
*A selection of interesting fruit and
equally interesting historical details
from one of America's great apple
revivalists. Includes tasting and
storage notes.*

Ball Blue Book Guide to Preserving,
various (Alltrista Consumer
Products, 2004)
*There are many editions of this,
from 1909 to 2015: they are all
excellent on bottling techniques,
procedures and recipes.*

The Book of Pears, Joan Morgan
(Ebury Press, 2015)
*An entertaining and comprehensive
history of a fruit described as "gold
to apple's silver". Recommended.*

Community Orchards Handbook,
Sue Clifford and Angela King
(Green Books, rev edn 2011)
*Everything you need to know about
planning, planting and managing an
orchard in any type of community.
From the organizers of Common
Ground and originators of Apple Day
and the Campaign for Local Distinc-
tiveness.*

Food for Free, Richard Mabey
(Collins, 2012)
*This classic has been inspiring
people for decades, and the updated
edition remains a valuable staple.*

*Food in Jars: Preserving in small
batches year-round*, Marisa
McClellan (Running Press, 2012)
*An excellent introduction to
preserving.*

The Fruit Tree Handbook, Ben
Pike (Green Books, 2011)
*Comprehensive and useful informa-
tion about planting and managing
apples, pears and other orchard fruit.*

*Getting Started with Growing
Fruit*, Gerry Edwards (National
Vegetable Society, 2015)
*A slim but interesting publication,
dripping with expertise.*

*Johnny Appleseed and the Ameri-
can Orchard: A cultural history*,
William Kerrigan (Johns Hopkins
University Press, 2012)
*Interesting and readable dig through
the mythology of this American
legend, the fruit he promoted and
the society in which he did so.*

The Modern Preserver, Kylee
Newton (Square Peg, 2015)
*Tasty ideas old and new, timeless
classics and on-trend flavours.*

The New Book of Apples, Joan
Morgan and Alison Richards
(Ebury Press, 2002)
*The most wide-ranging and defini-
tive history of apples ever. An
updated classic.*

The Story of the Apple, Barrie
Juniper and David Mabberley
(Timber Press, 2006)
*Addresses the question of whence
our sweet and varied domestic
apples arose, with the evidence from
DNA, geology, anthropology, archae-
ology, zoology and Classical history.
Now a bit of a collector's item!*

*The Thrifty Forager: Living off
your local landscape*, Alys Fowler
(Kyle Books, 2015)
*A thoroughly readable, common-
sense approach to the joys of foraging
in the twenty-first century.*

INDEX

ALSO BY GREEN BOOKS

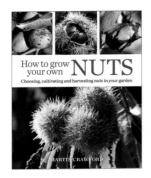

How to Grow Your Own Nuts:
Choosing, cultivating and harvesting nuts in your garden
Martin Crawford

A comprehensive book on all aspects of growing, harvesting, processing and using nuts, based on forest gardening principles. Filled with gorgeous images of trees and nuts on the branch, and of samples of nuts of different cultivars, this book is essential reading for any nut-loving gardener.

Nuts covered include old favourites such as chestnuts, hazelnuts and walnuts, as well as less common varieties such as pine nuts, hickories, butternuts and monkey-puzzle nuts.

The Fruit Tree Handbook
Ben Pike

A clear, practical guide for both amateur and expert, *The Fruit Tree Handbook* explains all you need to know in order to grow delicious fruit, from designing your orchard and planting your trees to harvesting your produce. It shows how to cultivate healthy trees through good management, and includes chapters on restoring an old orchard and setting up a community orchard. Whether you are planting a few trees in your garden or 50 trees in a field, this book provides the expert guidance you need to look after your trees – and be rewarded with basketfuls of luscious fruit at harvest time.

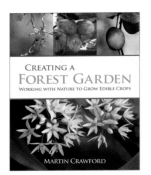

Creating a Forest Garden: Working with nature to grow edible crops
Martin Crawford

Forest gardening is a novel way of growing edible crops – with nature doing most of the work for you. Unlike in a conventional garden, there is little need for digging, weeding or pest control. Whether you just want to plant a small area in your garden or develop a larger plot, this book tells you everything you need to know. It gives detailed advice on planning, design, planting and maintenance, and includes a directory of over 500 plants: from trees to herbaceous perennials; root crops to climbers.

As well as more familiar plants you can grow your own chokeberries, goji berries, yams, heartnuts, bamboo shoots and buffalo currants – while creating a beautiful space that has great environmental benefits.

About Green Books

green books

Environmental publishers for 25 years.

For our full range of titles and to order direct from our website, see **www.greenbooks.co.uk**

Join our mailing list for new titles, special offers, reviews, author appearances and events:
www.greenbooks.co.uk/subscribe

For bulk orders (50+ copies) we offer discount terms. Contact **sales@greenbooks.co.uk** for details.

Send us a book proposal on eco-building, science, gardening, etc.: see **www.greenbooks.co.uk/for-authors**

 @ Green_Books   /GreenBooks